Biography

GW00496921

Matthew Perry

Laughing Through Pain

Chris Harrelson

TABLE OF CONTENTS

Introduction

INTRODUCTION

Hello, my name is Matthew, but you might know me by another name. My buddies refer to me as Matty.

You can think of what you're about to read as a communication from the beyond, my beyond.

It's the seventh day of the agony. I'm not talking about a stubbed toe or "The Whole Ten Yards." I capitalized Pain because it was the worst pain I'd ever felt—it was the Platonic Ideal of Pain, the model. I've heard that delivery is the greatest pain imaginable: this was the worst pain imaginable, but without the joy of holding a newborn in my arms at the end.

And then there are the sounds. The sounds, my God. Normally, I'm a fairly quiet, keep-to-myself type of guy. But on this particular night, I was yelling at the top of my lungs. Some nights, when the wind is right and all the cars are parked for the night, you can hear coyotes ripping apart something roaring in the Hollywood Hills. It sounds like children laughing in the distance at first, until you realize it's not—it's the foothills of death. Of course, the saddest thing is when the howling stops, because you know whatever was attacked is now dead. This is the pits.

I was staying in a sober living house in Southern California at the time. This came as no surprise given that I had spent half of my life in some type of treatment center or sober living house. Which is fantastic when you're twenty-four, but not so much when you're forty-two. I was 49 years old and still trying to get this monkey off my back.

By this point, I had learned more about drug addiction and alcoholism than any of the coaches or doctors I met at these facilities. Unfortunately, such self-awareness is useless. If the golden key to sobriety required hard work and knowledge, this beast would be little more than a hazy painful memory. I'd turned myself into a professional patient just to keep alive. Let us not sugarcoat things. I was still frightened of being alone at the age of 49. If I was left alone, my insane brain (mad only in one area, by the way) would find some reason to do the unthinkable: drink and do drugs. In light of the fact that doing this has damaged decades of my life, I'm frightened of doing it again. I have no fear of speaking in front of 20,000 people, but leave me alone on my couch in front of a TV for the night, and I become terrified. And that fear is of my own mind; fear of my own ideas; fear that my mind may once again encourage me to use drugs, as it has so many times before. I know my mind is out to murder me. I'm always filled with a latent loneliness, a yearning, clinging to the hope that something outside of myself will fix me. But I'd had enough of the outer world!

My girlfriend is Julia Roberts. It makes no difference; you must drink.

I recently purchased my ideal home, which has sweeping views of the entire city! You can't have that without a drug dealer.

I win if I make a million dollars per week, right? Do you want to drink something? Sure, I would. Thank you kindly.

I'd had everything. But it was all a con. Nothing was going to help. It would be years before I could even comprehend the concept of a solution. Please don't get me wrong. Julia, the dream mansion, and $1 million a week were all amazing, and I will be eternally grateful for all of them. I am one of the most fortunate men on the earth. And boy, did I have a good time.

I don't write this to make people feel sorry for me; I write it because it's true. I write these in case someone else is perplexed by the fact that they know they should stop drinking—they, like me, have all the facts and comprehend the consequences—but they still can't. My brothers and sisters, you are not alone. (There should be a picture of myself in the dictionary under the word "addict," looking around, perplexed.)

Despite Erin's comforting presence in the circumstances, I had many sleepless nights in Southern California. Sleep is a major challenge for me, particularly when I'm at one of these locations. Having said that, I don't think I've ever slept for more than four hours straight in my life. It didn't help that we'd been viewing nothing but prison documentaries—and I'd been on so much Xanax that my brain had fried to the point where I was convinced I was a real prisoner and this sober living facility was a real jail. My shrink's slogan is "reality is an acquired taste"—well, by that point, I'd lost both the taste and scent of reality; I'd Covid of the comprehension; I was utterly delusional.

I sat there, naked and in agony, wailing like a hound being ripped to shreds by coyotes. People in San Diego heard me, and Erin heard me. She emerged at the bathroom door, and as she looked down at my sad, naked form writhing in pain, she simply asked, "Do you want to go to the hospital?"

Erin dragged me out of the bath and dried me off. I started putting my clothes back on just as a counselor—presumably alerted by the slaughter of a dog on the premises—appeared at the door.

Catherine, the counselor, happened to be a lovely blond woman to whom I had supposedly proposed upon my arrival, so she wasn't exactly a favorite of mine. (I wasn't kidding when I said I'd asked her to marry me and then soon tumbled down a flight of stairs when we arrived.)

"This is just drug-seeking behavior," Catherine said to Erin as I finished getting dressed. "He's going to ask for drugs at the hospital."

We rushed past Catherine and Charles, out the door, and into the parking lot. I say "somehow" not because Catherine and Charles made a big deal about halting us, but because every time my feet touched the earth, the pain intensified.

Charles and Catherine had decided to step up their efforts to stop us and were now standing in front of the car, blocking us. Charles raised his hands, palms facing us, as if to cry "No!" as if three thousand pounds of automobile could be halted with the force of his mitts.

To make matters worse, Erin couldn't get the car started. Because, you know, I was on Friends, the ignition works by telling the car to start loudly. Catherine and the Palms refused to budge. Once she figured out how to start the wretched thing, there was only one thing left to do: Erin cranked the engine, shifted into drive, and slewed the car up and onto a curb—the jolt of that motion alone, ricocheting through my entire body, nearly killed me right there. She accelerated past Catherine and Charles and out into the street, two wheels up on the curb. They just stood there watching us drive away, but at this point I would have urged her to run over them—being unable to stop screaming is a terrifying situation to be in.

If all I was doing was getting drugs, I should have won an Oscar.

Saint John's Hospital was the nearest hospital to the sober house. Someone met us at the emergency valet since Erin had called ahead and informed them that a VIP was on her way. Erin had been concerned about my privacy when she made the call, not knowing how insanely unwell I was at the time. However, the hospital staff saw that something was gravely wrong and rushed me to a treatment room. "Erin, why are there Ping-Pong balls on the couch?" I was overheard saying.

When I was told I required surgery right away, every nurse in California descended on my room. "Get ready to run!" one of them said to Erin. Erin was ready, and we all sprinted—well, they ran; I was simply rolled to a procedure room at breakneck speed. Erin was ordered to leave seconds after I told her, "Please don't leave," and I closed my eyes, never to open again for two weeks.

When I went into a coma, the first thing that happened was that I aspirated into my breathing tube, vomiting ten days' worth of toxic excrement right into my lungs. My lungs didn't appreciate it (immediate pneumonia), and my gut erupted as a result. For those in the rear, let me repeat: my colon exploded! I've been accused of being a jerk before, but this time it was true.

At that moment, it seemed almost certain that I would die. Was it my bad luck that my colon exploded? Or was I just lucky that it happened in the one room in Southern California where they could intervene? In any case, I was now facing a seven-hour surgery, which allowed all of my loved ones plenty of time to rush to the hospital. When they arrived, they were each told, "Matthew has a two percent chance of making it through the night."

Everyone was overcome with emotion, and some collapsed right there in the hospital lobby. I'll have to live the rest of my life knowing that such statements were heard by my mother and others.

With me in surgery for at least seven hours and sure that the hospital would do all possible to save my life, my family and friends went home for the night to rest as my subconscious struggled for my life among the blades, tubes, and blood.

At UCLA, I was transferred to the heart and lung intensive care unit, which would become my home for the next six weeks. I was still in a coma, but I think I like it. What could be better than lying down, all curled up, and having medications pumped into me?

I've heard that when someone is seriously ill, a kind of detachment occurs—a "God only gives you what you can handle" type of thing kicks in. In the weeks following my coma, I refused to listen to anyone explain what had happened to me. I was too terrified that it was all my fault; that I had caused this to happen to myself. Instead of talking about it, I did the only thing I felt I could do: I immersed myself in family, spending hours with my wonderful sisters, Emily, Maria, and Madeline, who were hilarious, kind, and present. It was Erin at night; I was never alone again.

Maria, the hub of the Perry family (my mother being the hub of the Morrison side), eventually felt it was time to tell me what had transpired. I was bedridden, linked to fifty wires like a robot, as Maria filled me in. My worst fears had come true: I had done it; it was my fault.

However, things grew worse before they got better.

When I realized I was attracted to the therapist they assigned to me, I knew I was on my way back. True, I had a large scar on my stomach, but I was never the type of person who took his shirt off very often. I'm no Matthew McConaughey, and when I take a shower, I simply close my eyes.

As I already stated, I was never left alone in those hospitals during my whole time. As a result, there is light in the darkness. You only have to look hard enough to find it.

I was released after five extremely long months. Everything within me was supposed to heal in a year so that I could have a second surgery to remove the colostomy bag. But for the time being, we packed my overnight bags—five months of overnight—and returned home.

I'm also Batman.

Chapter 1
New York

Nobody ever expects something truly terrible to happen to them. Unless it does. Nobody survives a ruptured gut, aspiration pneumonia, or an ECMO machine. Until someone did it.
Me.

I keep returning to one simple, undeniable fact: I am alive. Given the chances, those three words are more remarkable than you might think; they have an unusual, gleaming look to me, like rocks returned from a distant planet. Nobody fully believes it. It's strange to live in a world where your death would shock everyone but surprise no one.

Above all, those three words—I am alive—fill me with a great sense of appreciation. When you've been as near to the divine as I have, you don't really have a choice about gratitude: it's like a coffee-table book on your living room table—you barely notice it, but it's there. But there's a persistent anguish shadowing that thankfulness, buried deep someplace in the faint-anise-distant-licorice of the Diet Coke and filling my lungs like every drag of every cigarette.

But, you see, I can't answer the question "Why?" when I feel insufficient. You can't give something away, something you don't have. And most of the time, I have nagging thoughts like, "I'm not enough, I don't matter, I'm too needy." These thoughts make me uneasy. I need love, yet I'm afraid of it. If I drop my Chandler and reveal to you who I am, you might notice me, but even worse, you might notice me and leave me. That is something I cannot have. I'm not going to make it. Not any longer. It will demolish me and turn me into a bit of dust.

So I'll start with you. I'll make up a story in my head about something going wrong with you, and I'll believe it. And then I'll leave. But there can't be anything wrong with all of them, Matso. What is the common factor here?

And now I've got these scars on my tummy. These shattered love affairs. Rachel is leaving. (No, it's not that one. Rachel as she is. Rachel, the ex-girlfriend of my fantasies.) They torment me as I lie awake at 4:00 a.m. in my Pacific Palisades home with a view. I'm 52 years old. It's no longer as adorable.

Every home I've ever had has had a view. That is the most crucial aspect for me.

I was five years old when I was put on a plane from Montreal, Canada, where I lived with my mother, to Los Angeles, California, to visit my father. I was an "unaccompanied minor" (which was also the title of this book at one point). It was common practice to put children on flights at the time—flying children alone at that age was just something people did. It was wrong, but they did it. For a fraction of a second, I thought it would be a thrilling experience, but then I realized I was too young to be alone, and this was all absolutely horrifying (and nonsense). Come pick me up, one of you! I was five years old. Is everyone insane?

When you fly as an unaccompanied minor, you receive a tiny sign around your neck that says UNACCOMPANYED MINOR, as well as early boarding, kids-only lounges, goodies up the ying-yang, someone to walk you to the plane... Maybe it should have been fantastic (later, as a celebrity, I got all these privileges and more at airports, but they reminded me of that first flight, so I loathed them). The flight attendants were meant to care for me, but they were too busy distributing champagne in coach (as was customary in the 1970s). Because the two-drink limit had lately been eliminated, the flight seemed like six hours in Sodom and Gomorrah. The stink of alcohol pervaded the room; the guy next to me had at least ten old-fashioneds. (After a few hours, I quit counting.) I couldn't comprehend why any grownup would want to drink the same drink repeatedly... Ah, childhood.

I was scared as hell. I attempted to read my Highlights magazine, but every time the plane shook in the air, I knew I was going to die. I had no one to tell me everything was fine, no one to look to for confidence. My feet didn't even touch the ground. I was too terrified to recline the seat and take a nap, so I just sat there, waiting for the next bump, imagining what it would be like to fall 35,000 feet.

I didn't fall, at least not in the literal sense. The jet eventually began its descent into the lovely California evening. I could see the lights twinkling, streets strewn out like a great sparkling magic carpet, wide swaths of dark I now know were the hills, the city pulsing up toward me as I plastered my little face against the plane window, and I remember thinking that those lights, and all that beauty, meant I was about to become a parent.

One of the numerous factors that contributed to a lifelong sense of abandonment was the absence of a parent on the flight.... They wouldn't have left me alone if I'd been good enough, right? Isn't that how it's meant to work? The other children were accompanied by their parents. I had a sign and a magazine with me.

So, whenever I buy a new house—and there have been many (never underestimate the power of geography), it has to have a view. I want to be able to look down on safety, somewhere where someone is thinking of me, somewhere where there is affection. Parenting takes place someplace in that valley, or in that wide ocean beyond the Pacific Coast Highway, on the gleaming primaries of the red-tail's wings. That's where you'll find love. That is where I call home. I can now relax.

I've spent a significant amount of my life in hospitals. Being in hospitals makes even the strongest of us feel sorry for ourselves, and I've made a concerted effort to feel sorry for myself. Every time I lie there, I find myself reflecting on my life, twisting each moment this way and that, like a perplexing find at an archeological dig, trying to figure out why I had spent so much of my life in misery and emotional pain. I could always tell where the genuine agony was coming from. (I'd always known why I was in physical discomfort at the time—the explanation was, you can't drink that much, asshole.)

We've arrived at the fifth annual Miss Canadian University Snow Queen pageant, which is "judged on intelligence, participation in student activities, personality, and personality as well as beauty." To celebrate the arrival of a new Miss CUSQ, the Canadians planned a "torchlight parade with floats, bands, and the contestants," as well as "an outdoor cookout and a hockey game."

Suzanne Langford is one of the eleven candidates for the award, and she represents the University of Toronto. Against her have been arrayed beauties with wonderful names such as Ruth Shaver from British Columbia, Martha Quail from Ottawa, and even Helen "Chickie" Fuhrer from McGill, who presumably added the "Chickie" to compensate for the fact that her surname was a tad unfortunate just two decades after World War II ended.

Suzanne Langford was overjoyed when John Perry remained the night, and a year or two later, after the montage scene, she found herself in Williamstown, Massachusetts, where John is from, and cells within her were splitting and conquering. Who knows what went wrong in those simple divisions—all I know is that addiction is an illness, and like my parents when they met, I didn't stand a fucking chance.

I was born on August 19, 1969, a Tuesday, the son of former Serendipity Singers member John Bennett Perry and former Miss Canadian University Snow Queen Suzanne Marie Langford. The night I came, there was a massive storm (of course there was); everyone was playing Monopoly while waiting for me (of course they were). I arrived on Earth around a month after the Moon landing and one day after Woodstock—so, somewhere between the cosmic purity of the heavenly spheres and all that shitdown at Yasgur's Farm, I became life, interfering with someone's chance to build motels on Boardwalk.

I was told I took phenobarbital between the ages of thirty and sixty days throughout the second month of my existence. This is a critical period in a baby's growth, particularly when it comes to sleeping. (Fifty years later, I still have trouble sleeping.) I'd just conk out once the barbiturate kicked in. Apparently, I'd be crying, and the medicine would kick in, knocking me unconscious, causing my father to burst out laughing. He wasn't being mean; stoned babies are amusing. I have newborn images of myself where I'm fully zonked, nodding like an addict at the age of seven weeks. Which, I suppose, is curiously suitable for a child born the day after Woodstock ended.

"OK" is a distant memory or something reserved for Hallmark cards while I'm detoxing. I'm pleading like a child for any kind of drug that may help ease the symptoms—a grown guy pleading for relief while presumably looking wonderful on the cover of People magazine. I'd give up everything—every car, every house, all my money—just to put a stop to it. And when detox is finally over, you are ecstatic, pledging to yourself that you would never put yourself through it again. Until you find yourself in the same situation three weeks later.

Around my ninth month, my parents decided they'd had enough of each other, hid me in a car seat in Williamstown, and the three of us drove five and a half hours to the Canadian border. I can almost hear the stillness of the vehicle journey. Of course, I didn't say anything, and the two ex-lovers in the front seat had had enough of each other. Despite this, the quiet must have been deafening. Something huge was going on. My maternal grandfather, the military-like Warren Langford, was waiting for us there, pacing up and down, stamping his feet to keep warm, or in frustration, or both. He'd be waving at us as we drew up, as if we were about to start on some sort of fantastic vacation. I would have been delighted to see him, but my father is said to have taken me out of my car seat, handed me into the arms of my grandfather, and then discreetly abandoned me and my mother. Then Mom got out of our car, and my mother and I stood there, listening to the waters hurtle over the Falls and roar into the Niagara Gorge, while my father sped away, forever.

My father drove away, who knows where. He did not return from work on the first or second day. I was expecting he'd come home in three days, then a week, then a month, but after about six weeks, I gave up. I was too young to know where California was, never alone what it meant to "go follow his dream of being an actor"—what the fuck is an actor? And where the hell is my father?

My father, who subsequently became a fantastic father, was leaving his kid with a twenty-one-year-old lady he knew was far too young to manage a child on her own. My mother is wonderful and emotional, and she was simply too young for this. She, too, had been abandoned in the parking lot of the border crossing between the United States and Canada. My mother became pregnant with me when she was twenty, and by the time she was twenty-one and a new mother, she was divorced. I would have tried to drink it if I had had a baby at the age of twenty-one. She did her best, which says a lot about her, but she simply wasn't ready for the burden, and I wasn't ready to deal with anything, having only recently been born.

Mom and I were both abandoned before we really got to know each other.

Someone slammed a door on my hand when I was in kindergarten, and after the enormous sparkles of blood stopped arcing out like fireworks, someone thought to bandage me up and take me to the hospital. It was obvious that I had indeed lost the tip of my middle finger. My mother was summoned and hurried to the hospital. She walked in sobbing (understandably) and found me on a gurney with a massive bandage on my hand. I interrupted her with, "You don't need to cry—I didn't cry."

There hasn't been much change. If you give me all the OxyContin I can handle, I'll feel taken care of, and when I'm taken care of, I'll be able to take care of everyone else and look outside and serve someone. But without medication, I believe I would sputter away into oblivion. This, of course, means that I can't be useful or in service in a relationship since I'm just trying to get to the next minute, hour, or day. There's the fear sickness, the sense of inadequacy. A little of this, a little of that, and I'm fine—you don't taste anything when you're high.

I didn't have a father or all ten fingers, but I did have a quick intellect and a quick mouth even back then. When you combine that with a mother who was really busy and important, as well as having a quick mind and mouth... Well, let's just say it didn't go well. It's worth noting that I was never given enough attention—no matter what Mom did, it was never enough. And don't forget that she was doing the work of two people at the same time, while poor old dad was in LA battling with his own problems and ambitions.

Suzanne Perry (who used her father's name professionally) was a spinmeister, similar to Allison Janney from The West Wing. She worked as the press secretary for Pierre Trudeau, the Canadian prime leader at the time and an avid traveler. (The Toronto Star captioned a photo of the two of them, "Press aide Suzanne Perry works for one of Canada's best-known men—Prime Minister Pierre Trudeau—but she is quickly becoming a celebrity herself; simply by appearing at his side." Consider yourself a celebrity simply by standing next to Pierre Trudeau. He was the sophisticated, well-connected Prime Minister who had dated Barbra Streisand, Kim Cattrall, Margot Kidder... His ambassador in Washington reportedly complained that he'd invited three different girlfriends to a dinner, so there was a lot of spinning required for a man so enamored of women. My mother's job required her to be away from home frequently, leaving me to compete for attention with the continuous worries of a large Western democracy and its charismatic, swashbuckling leader. (At the time, I believe the phrase was "latchkey kid"—a bland word for being left fucking alone.) As a result, I learned to be funny (pratfalls, quick one-liners, you know the drill) because I had to—my mother was stressed by her stressful job, and she was already highly emotional (and abandoned), and my being funny tended to calm her down enough that she would cook some food, sit down at the dinner table with me, and hear me out, after I had heard her out. But I'm not going to blame her for working—someone had to bring home the bacon. It just meant that I spent a lot of time alone. (I used to tell people I was a lonely child because I had misheard the words "only child.")

I've always been left behind. So much so that when a plane flew over our house in Ottawa, I used to ask my grandma, "Is my mother on that plane?" because I was always afraid she'd disappear like my father (she never did). My mother is stunning; she was the center of attention in every area she entered. And she is unquestionably the source of my hilarity.

With Dad away in California, Mom, who was gorgeous, smart, personable, and the center of attention in every room she entered, would date men, and they'd date her back, and sure enough, I'd transform every one of those men into my father. When a plane flew over our house, I'd once again ask my grandma, "Is that [Michael] [Bill] [John] [insert name of Mom's latest beau] flying away?" I was constantly losing my father and being abandoned at the border. The roar of the Niagara River was always in my ears, and not even phenobarbital could silence it. My grandma would coo at me and crack open a can of Diet Coke, the faint-anise and distant-licorice flavoring my taste receptors with sorrow.

When he returned to Canada, the image of his face and the smell of his apartment faded with time. Then it would be my birthday again, and my mother would do everything she could to compensate for the fact that my father wasn't there, and when the too-large cake appeared, covered in many dripping candles, each year I'd wish for one thing: I want my parents to get back together. Maybe if my family life had been more solid, if my father had been present, if he hadn't been Superman, if I hadn't had a quick mind and mouth, if Pierre Trudeau... I wouldn't be so miserable all the time.

Sitting with my mother and watching that movie is my absolute favorite childhood memory. But now the Prime Minister of Canada was calling, and I was about to lose my mother for the second time. As she answered the phone, I heard her use her professional, spinmeister-like voice; the sound of a different person, Suzanne Perry, in fact, not my mother.

I remember seeing my mother in the kitchen crying about this time and wondering, "Why doesn't she just drink?" I'm not sure where I got the idea that an alcoholic drink would make me stop sobbing. I hadn't had a drink by eight o'clock (I'd have to wait another six years!), but the culture all around me had taught me that drinking equaled laughing and having fun, as well as a much-needed escape from sorrow. Why didn't Mom just drink since she was crying? She'd be intoxicated and wouldn't feel as much, right?

Maybe she was crying because we were constantly moving— Montreal, Ottawa, Toronto—even though I spent the majority of my childhood in Ottawa. I spent a lot of time alone; nannies came and went, but they never stayed long enough for me to add them to the list of individuals who abandoned me.... I just kept being humorous, snappy, and smart-mouthed in order to live.

We were back in Ottawa by sixth grade, where we belonged. I was starting to understand the power of making others laugh. In between being the class cutup at Ashbury College, my all-boys secondary school in Ottawa, I landed the role of Rackham, "the fastest gun in the West," in a play called The Death and Life of Sneaky Fitch, put on by the school's acting instructor, Greg Simpson. It was a significant part, and I loved it—making people laugh was important to me. All those parents appeared to be interested in their children's activities until—wham!—that Perry youngster really made people laugh. (Of all the medicines, that one is still the most effective in terms of making me happy.) Being the star of The Death and Life of Sneaky Fitch was very beneficial since it provided me with something to strive for.

Despite the fact that I was now a big brother, I was still the bad kid. One year, before Christmas, I went through all the closets to see what my gifts were; I was also stealing money, smoking more and more, and getting worse and worse grades. Because I talked so much and spent so much time trying to make people laugh, the teachers once turned my desk so that it faced the back wall of the classroom. Dr. Webb, one of my teachers, once stated, "If you don't change the way you are, you'll never amount to anything." (Should I reveal that when I got the People magazine cover, I had a copy sent to Dr. Webb with the comment, "I guess you were wrong"? That would be impolite.)

For real-world matches, I went to Rockcliffe Lawn Tennis Club in Ottawa. At the club, you had to dress all white. There used to be a sign in front of the club that said WHITES ONLY, but someone worried it could give the incorrect idea. (After hastily changing the sign to WHITE DRESS ONLY, everyone moved on.) There were eight courts, primarily populated by seniors, and I would spend the entire day waiting in the clubhouse in case someone didn't show up and a fourth court was required and I could fill in. The older generation adored me because I could catch every ball, but I also had a wild temper. I'd throw my racket, curse, and become enraged, and if I was losing badly, I'd start bawling. This generally happened before I came back to win—I'd be one set down, 5-1 down, love-40 down, bawling, and then I'd win in three. I'd be crying the whole time, but I'd be thinking, I'm going to win; I know I'm going to win. Others were less concerned about winning.

When I was fourteen, I had my first drink. I waited as long as I could.

We were all hanging out in my backyard one night. Nobody was home; the sun streamed through the clouds above, and none of us realized that something really crucial was about to happen. I was sleeping in the grass and mud of Canada, knowing nothing.
Could I be more oblivious?

We made the decision to drink. I'm not sure who had the notion, and none of us realized what we were getting ourselves into. We had a six-pack of Budweiser and a bottle of Andrès Baby Duck white wine. The Murrays took the beer, while I took the wine. By the way, this was all in broad daylight—we were in my backyard. My parents were not at home, which was a surprise, so we left.

All of the alcohol had been consumed within fifteen minutes. The Murrays were puking all around me, and I was just lying on the grass when something occurred to me. That thing that distinguishes me physically and psychologically from my peers occurred. I was resting back in the grass and mud, watching the moon, surrounded by fresh Murray puke, when I realized that nothing troubled me for the first time in my life. The universe made sense; it wasn't twisted and insane. I felt complete and at ease. I'd never been happier than I was at that time. This is it, I thought; this is what I've been looking for. This is probably how most people feel all the time. I don't have any issues. It's all gone now. I don't require any attention. I'm fine, I'm taken care of.

Things at home continued to deteriorate. Keith had created a fantastic new family for my mother. Emily came, and she was as blond as a pin. And, like Caitlin, I fell in love with her right away. However, I was frequently on the outside looking in, still that kid in the clouds on an unsupervised flight somewhere else. Mom and I were constantly arguing; tennis was the only place I felt happy, and even when I won, I was upset or sobbing. What was a guy to do?

Yes, Los Angeles, my father, and a new life were all calling, but I was fifteen, and leaving would disrupt my family life and break my mother's heart. But she never asked if it was okay for me to marry Keith, relocate to Toronto, and have two children.... And in Canada, I was upset, sobbing, and drinking, and my mother and I were bickering, and I wasn't a full member of the family, and I sucked at school, and who knew if I'd have to move soon anyway, and on and on and on. And, for God's sake, a child wants to know who his father is.

I made the decision to go. My parents had talked about it and pondered if moving to LA would be better for my tennis career in any case. (Little did I realize that the best I'd be in Southern California would be a solid club player, the standard being so much higher in a place where you can play 365 days a year, as compared to Canada, where you're lucky if you get a couple of months before the permafrost appears.) Even with that thought, my decision to go shattered the fabric of my family.

My mother was nice enough to drive me to the airport early the next morning, despite what must have been a painful drive for her, and watch me fly away from her for the rest of her life. I'm not sure how I mustered the guts to go on this journey. I'm still not sure if it was the correct thing to do.

I flew to Los Angeles, still an unaccompanied minor, but a pro by now, to meet my father. I was so afraid that even the glitz and glam of Hollywood couldn't calm me down. But I'd soon see the lights of the metropolis and have a parent again.

When I went home from the hospital after five months, the first thing I did was start a cigarette. After all that time, the inhalation, the smoke streaming into my lungs, felt just like the first cigarette I'd ever had in my life. It was like returning home for the second time.

I was no longer in agony—the extensive surgery on my stomach had resulted in scar tissue, which made my stomach feel like I was doing a sit-up at full stretch all the time, but it wasn't pain. It was more of a bother.

After my colon exploded, I had my first operation and had to wear a really gorgeous colostomy bag—a look even I couldn't pull off. A second surgery to remove the bag was scheduled, but in the interim, I was prohibited from smoking (smokers tend to have significantly uglier scars, hence the restriction). Not to mention that I was missing my two front teeth—a bite into a piece of peanut butter toast had fractured them, and I hadn't had time to repair them.

When I arrived in treatment, they gave me Subutex for the detox, so it wasn't too horrible. I entered my room and the clock began to tick. By day four, I was completely out of my mind; this had always been the most difficult day. I also knew how serious they were going to take this smoking business. It was determined that I could smoke while in detox, but after I got to the third floor, I couldn't.

They insisted so much that I was locked inside the premises and unable to leave. I was on the third floor, and all around me, New York purred in the distance, going about its business and loving life while their favorite sardonic comedy star was in hell for the umpteenth time. If I listened closely enough, I could hear the subway—the F train, the R train, the 4, 5, 6—deep beneath me, or perhaps it was the rattling of something else, something unexpected, scary, and relentless.

I was convinced that this treatment was a prison. A genuine prison, not the one I had imagined previously. Red bricks and black iron railings. I'd somehow ended up in jail. I'd never broken the law—or, more accurately, I'd never been caught—yet here I was, in lockup, pokey, the House of D. I even looked like a felon with my two front teeth missing, and every counselor was a guard. They could have fed me via a slot in a locked door.

Chapter 2
Another Generation Shot to Hell

That was the year of the Los Angeles Olympic Games, when a hundred thousand people packed the Coliseum and the Rose Bowl, where Mary Lou Retton needed a 10 to win the gymnastics all-around and nailed it, and Carl Lewis won four gold medals by running really fast and jumping really far.

It was also the year I moved to America, a lost Canadian boy with a dick that didn't seem to work, on his way to Hollywood to live with his father.

Before I went, a girl tried to have sex with me in Ottawa, but I was so scared that I drank six beers beforehand and couldn't perform. I'd been drinking for a few years by then, ever since I gave my mother away to that gorgeous man, Keith.

I didn't make the connection between the alcohol and my private parts not working. And no one could possibly be aware of this—no one. So I was wandering throughout the world thinking that sex was only for other people. For quite some time; years. Sex sounded like a lot of fun, but it wasn't in my arsenal. This meant that I was (con)genitally impotent, at least in my head and pants.

Sports were also part of the initial plan for me. My tennis had progressed to the point that we considered enrolling me at Nick Bollettieri's Tennis Academy in Florida. Bollettieri was the leading tennis coach, having worked with Monica Seles, Andre Agassi, Maria Sharapova, and Venus and Serena Williams, among many others, but once in LA, it became clear that I was only going to be a perfectly solid club player. I remember entering a satellite tournament in front of my dad and my new family (he'd remarried Debbie, a gorgeous woman and the catch of the century, in 1980, and they had a very little daughter, Maria), and losing my first match.

It was time to hunt for a new job.

Another of my medicines was acting. And it didn't cause the damage that alcohol was already causing. In fact, waking up after a night of drinking was becoming increasingly difficult. Not during the school day—it hadn't gotten that far yet. But, without a doubt, every weekend.

I was the pale Canadian kid with a quick mouth, and there's something about being an outsider that intrigues teenagers—we seem exotic, especially if we have a Canadian accent and can identify the whole Toronto Maple Leafs lineup. Plus, my father was the Old Spice guy; for years, my classmates had seen Dad dressed as a sailor on shore leave—complete with peacoat and black sailor cap—slinging that iconic white bottle at clean-shaven bit actors while imploring them to "Clean up your life with Old Spice!" It wasn't Shakespeare, but he was renowned enough, tall and attractive, and extremely amusing, and he was my father.

Dad was a drinker as well. Every evening, he'd return home from whatever set he'd been on, or not, pour himself a large slug of vodka tonic, and declare, "This is the best thing that's happened to me all day."

But there was a significant difference. Dad would be up at seven o'clock every morning, bright and breezy; he'd shower and apply his aftershave (never Old Spice), and head off to the bank or his agency or set—he never missed a thing. Dad exemplified the term "functional drinker." I, on the other hand, was battling to wake up and raising whispers among those drinking around me.

The drink and the walk left a chasm in me that I'm still dealing with. I was so troubled; I was such a messed up guy. All I'd done was what Sigal had done—I'd come to Los Angeles, along with gymnasts and sprinters and horses and authors and actors and wannabes and has-beens and Old Spice actors, and now a big emptiness had opened up beneath me. I was standing on the rim of a huge pit of fire, similar to "The Pit of Hell" in Turkmenistan's Karakum Desert. The drink and the walk had created a thinker, a seeker, but not some soft-focus, Buddhist nonsense—one who was on the edge of a deep crater of flames, haunted by the lack of answers, being alone, wanting love but being terrified of abandonment, wanting excitement but being unable to appreciate it, by a dick that didn't work. A fifteen-year-old lad was brought up close to the face of eschatology, so close he could smell the vodka on his breath. I was face-to-face with the four last things: death, judgment, heaven, and hell.

Years later, my father would take his own momentous walk: he had a bad night on the booze and went through some bushes or something, and the next morning he told Debbie about it, and she said, "Is this the way you want to live your life?" And he replied no, then went for a stroll, stopped drinking, and hasn't had a drop since.

By 1986, I was convinced that celebrity would change everything, and I want it more than anyone else on the earth. It was exactly what I needed. It was the one thing that could make me whole again. I was sure of it. When I lived in Los Angeles, I would periodically run across a superstar, such as Billy Crystal at the Improv, or Nicolas Cage at the adjacent booth, and I knew they had no difficulties—in fact, all of their troubles had been washed away. They were well-known.

I'd been auditioning regularly and had even landed a couple of roles, most notably in the first season of Charles in Charge. "My father's a Princeton man, and a surgeon—I'd like to follow in his footsteps!" I played Ed, a preppy, plaid-sweater-and-tie-wearing square who boldly intoned his one main line. But there was work and TV, and before I knew it, I was skipping school to hang out in diners with females who enjoyed my accent and fast banter and my burgeoning TV career and my ability to listen to them. I knew I could listen to and aid women in trouble because of my training back in Canada. (If you're a woman in distress and you sing a song about it, I'll listen to it over and over.) So there I was, holding court with a gaggle of young women, quick with a line and a smirk and a willing ear; I'd ditched the preppy, Charles in Charge look as soon as I left the Universal lot in Studio City and was dressed like any cool teen in the mid-1980s: denim jacket over a plaid shirt, or probably wearing a Kinks T-shirt before going home to listen to Air Supply.

Days seem long when you're nearly sixteen, especially when you're charming a group of young women in a Hollywood greasy spoon. As I was joking about, a middle-aged man strolled past the booth and placed a message on a napkin in front of me on the table, then walked away and right out the door. The females all stopped talking; I peered at the guy's back as he walked away, then did a mock-up of Chandler's double take, which elicited additional laughter.

Richert had seen me perform for the ladies in the 101 that day and had watched enough of The Matthew Perry Show to want to cast me in a film based on his novel A Night in the Life of Jimmy Reardon. The novel and film are set in Chicago in the early 1960s; Reardon is a teenager who is being forced to go business school when all he really wants to do is save up enough money to fly to Hawaii to visit his love. I was cast as Reardon's best buddy, Fred Roberts, who, like Ed in Charles in Charge, was well-off and a little snobbish, as well as suffering from chronic virginity. (I can sympathize.) I abandoned the preppy appearance once more, since Fred was to wear a gray felt flat cap and leather jacket over a formal shirt and tie, as well as black leather gloves. The character of Reardon sleeps with my girlfriend in the film, but that's fine since playing Reardon would be a luxury to be cheated on by.

The film was shot in Chicago, so there I was, seventeen years old and on my way to the Windy City, sans parents, sans anything, an unaccompanied minor once more, but this time it seemed like liberation, like what I was born to do. I'd never been so ecstatic in my life. I fell completely in love with acting in Chicago, on this film, and with River Phoenix—and the icing on top of this profoundly amazing experience was that River and I became fast friends. On North Rush Street, he and I drank beer and played pool (The Color of Money had just come out, and pool was the thing to do). We had a per diem; we flirted with girls, albeit that was the extent of my involvement since, well, you know.

River was a lovely man on the inside and out—too lovely for this world, it turned out. It always seems to be the most brilliant players who fail. Why do creative thinkers like River Phoenix and Heath Ledger die while Keanu Reeves lives on? River was a greater actress than I was, but I was more amusing. But, looking back decades later, I certainly held my own in our sequences. But, more importantly, River saw the world in a different way than we all did, which made him intriguing, engaging, and, yes, gorgeous, but not in a Gap ad kind of way (though he was that, too)—in a there-is-no-one-else-like-him sort of way. Not to mention he was on his way to stardom and you'd never know it.

Our film would eventually bomb at the box office, but that didn't matter. Even if it was just North Rush Street in cold Chicago, we'd been somewhere lovely and fantastic. And I knew that was the best experience of my life. My work was completed in approximately three weeks, but they (most likely River) liked me so much that they kept me on the film till the conclusion. Things didn't get any better after that.

I cried again seven years later, on Halloween 1993, in front of the Viper Room in West Hollywood, when River died. (I heard screams from my apartment, went back to bed, and awoke to the news.) "The spirits of [River's] generation are being worn down," his mother wrote after his death, referring to drug usage, and by then, I was drinking every night. But it would be years before I realized what she meant.

I went back to LA from Chicago with Jimmy Reardon in the bag and returned to planet Earth in the guise of high school. I was still auditioning for a lot of stuff, but I wasn't getting anywhere. I was largely booking comedies, but I ended up guest starring on almost everything. My grades, however, remained dismal. I graduated with a 2.0 grade point average. My only request at my graduation was that both my mother and father attend, which they gladly fulfilled. The terribly awkward supper that followed appeared to just emphasize the notion that the child they shared was bound to be uncomfortable by default, despite being the funniest person in the room most of the time. But that night at dinner, I was just the third most attractive and third most funny. At the very least, a boyhood dream of theirs had come true, if only for one night, and even then, only in awkward silences and barbs handed back and forth like some angry cosmic joint.

Tricia had disrobed both of us and brought us into bed before this little conversation could evolve into a threepenny opera. I recall the foothills of lovemaking as absolute ecstasy, but like a newbie mountaineer, I worried that once I passed a certain base camp, no amount of oxygen would let me climb any higher. And so it turned out. What else can I say?—I couldn't get that item to work properly. I considered everything, spinning intricate, sensual ideas through my jumbled mind, hoping to hit upon something—one thing, that'll do!—that would solidify my commitment to future joy. Nothing worked; nothing worked. I padded my thin, nude body over to a chair in the apartment, terrified yet again, abandoning Tricia Fisher's kind arms. (You could easily bend me in half if you wanted to.) I sat there, soft and sorrowful, my two hands cupped over my lap like a nun's during Vespers, trying to hide my embarrassment and perhaps a tear or two.

I eventually relaxed and took a long breath. "Come with me," Tricia stated calmly and simply. That will never happen again."

With that, she approached me, took my hand, led me back to bed, laid me down, and sure enough... absolute glory for two solid minutes! That night, thanks to a miracle world and the efforts of a lovely young woman who deserved better, I misplaced then lost my virginity, and impotence has never been part of my lexicon since, just as she promised. Everything about me, at least physically, works perfectly.

I'm still learning about sex. I immediately agreed. We arrived at my apartment, and as we approached the door, she stopped me and shouted, "Wait, wait, wait!" This is impossible for me! You must take me home."

The next day, I was troubled by what had transpired, and since I was already in treatment, I told my therapist about it.

I was eighteen at the time; I am fifty-two today, and he has always been correct. I've cheated a little by leaving a pair of shoes on my doorstep as a kind of indication that this is where the shoes go. But that therapist's intuition has always been correct—if a woman keeps her shoes on, it's a make-out session at best.)

Years later, while Friends was at its peak, Tricia and I would date again. She didn't abandon me, but old worries surfaced, and I called it quits. I only wish I could fully feel and know that mom did not abandon me. Perhaps things would be better. Perhaps vodka tonic would not have become my preferred beverage.

But I want to thank Tricia and those that came after her. And I genuinely apologize from the bottom of my heart to all the women I abandoned merely because I was worried they would leave me. If only I'd known what I know now....

I was also in Don't Look Up at one point, and despite the fact that I was on my way to recovery in Switzerland, I went to Boston to film my scene. While there, I pitched a line to Adam that he loved and which became the knockout punch to the scene, which is always the goal (he ended up not utilizing the scene—shit happens; no big deal). That is, Adam McKay and I got along great, and here he was, liking my pitch.

I was in pain from the scar tissue from the operations at the time, so I required pain relievers, but I'd become hooked to them, which would only cause further damage to my insides... But now that I'm feeling a little better, I was delighted to receive a call from Adam. We were just chatting, but there's no such thing as simply chatting in Hollywood, so I decided what the hell—why is he phoning me? And since he never appeared to get to his point, I took advantage of the situation and pitched him my proposal.

I, too, have a history with this nonsense. Years before, when Bruce Willis received the People's Choice Award for Best Actor for The Sixth Sense, he requested me to give it to him. Backstage that night, I met Haley Joel Osment and M. Night Shyamalan, and we spoke for approximately 10 minutes.

I never do this since I've been burnt far too many times by this line of thinking, but I started having wild fantasies about what this could do for my career. He mentioned another bar that had recently opened across town and asked if I wanted to go with him. Did I want to accompany him? M. Night Fucking' Shyamalan! Of course, I wanted to accompany him.

We walked to the valet, got in our cars, and I accompanied him across town to this new place, convinced that I would be the star of his next major movie—yeah, there was going to be a new, amazing, twisting movie, and the trick ending would be me!

My mind was spinning in circles. I'm not sure why—he just appeared to appreciate me and my work, and I was drunk enough to believe that this was going to be a life-changing night. As we took our seats at the new location, I felt comfortable [read: inebriated] enough to suggest that we collaborate on anything. All of a sudden, an odd look crossed his face, and I immediately regretted saying it. He excused himself to visit the restroom, and while he was gone, someone I recognized came up to me and inquired about my night.

Turns out, "M. Night" was just an Indian gentleman who resembled M. Night Shyamalan (or was it N. Night Shyamalan?), and who was, in fact, the maître d' at Mr. Chow Beverly Hills, a hip restaurant in LA that I used to frequent... and that I no longer do, because I told its maître d' that we should work together someday. What type of night did he expect to have? I pondered.

Chapter 3
Baggage

Every evening, my friends and I would go to the Formosa Café on Santa Monica Boulevard in West Hollywood. There were two signs over the bar: one under all the headshots that said where the stars dine, and the other said where the stars eat. The other said wine by the glass, but we didn't drink by the glass—we drank by the pint, quart, and gallon... and vodka rather than wine.

I first met Hank when I was sixteen. We were auditioning for a pilot starring Ellen Greene (from Little Shop of Horrors) on the CBS lot. He played my uncle in the pilot, and we both were cast. We got along so well that when it was time for me to leave the nest, I moved into a studio apartment in his building. He was already a seriously humorous guy when I met him, and he was doing a lot of voiceover work by the time I met him. That employment would eventually lead to him becoming extremely wealthy, but at the time, all we wanted was fame. All we wanted was fame, celebrity, fame. And, uh, females and, uh, fame. It was all we cared about because, at least for me, I thought being famous would fill the huge emptiness that was developing inside of me all the time.

That night was the first time I became obsessed with drinking. No one else seemed to be bothered by Gaby's lack of drink—but I had that overpowering pull, like a giant magnet and I was just little shards of iron. This terrified me, especially since it appeared to be simply me who was struggling. So I resolved not to go out and get more to drink that night... but it left me unable to sleep, restless, tossing and turning, and completely lost to it. Until the light came up, I was restless, angry, and dissatisfied.

Ten years later, I read in the Big Book of Alcoholics Anonymous, "Drinkers think they are trying to escape, but they are really trying to overcome a mental disorder they didn't know they had."

Someone finally understands me. But reading that was both fantastic and terrifying. It meant I wasn't alone—there were others who felt the same way I did—but it also meant I was an alcoholic who would have to stop drinking one day at a time for the rest of my life.

It made me want to be someone completely different. It seemed difficult to quit. Learning to live without it was akin to expecting someone to go about his or her day without breathing. I shall be eternally grateful to alcohol for this. It ultimately beat me down to a respectable state.

According to Malcolm Gladwell, if you do something for ten thousand hours, you can become an expert. As a result, I became an expert in two areas: 1980s tennis and drinking. Only one of the topics is critical enough to save a life.

Surprisingly, I'd portrayed a character named Azarian in Beverly Hills, 90210. It was a major deal to get a guest slot on episode nineteen of the twenty-two-episode inaugural season. Beverly Hills, 90210 hadn't yet achieved cultural phenomenon status when I played Roger Azarian, Beverly Hills High tennis star and the son of a hard-charging, distant businessman father—but the themes in that episode (teen depression, suicide, and learning disabilities) distinguished it as a show that wouldn't shy away from real shit, no matter how privileged its setting.

Second Chance had a terrific premise: a forty-year-old man named Charles Russell dies in a hovercraft accident (which happens all the time) and goes to meet Saint Peter in his office. If the light shines gold on Charles as he stands in judgment, he goes to paradise; if it shines red, he goes to hell; but if it shines blue, as it did in Mr. Russell's case, he was dubbed a Blue Lighter, which means they had no idea what to do with him. So Saint Peter sends him back to Earth to meet his fifteen-year-old self and coach him through a life of wiser decisions. That way, when he boards a hovercraft for the second time at forty, when he dies for the second time because he's been a better guy, the light will shift from a we're-not-sure-what-to-do-with-you blue to a we're-sold, welcome-to-eternity gold. Can you think of a better setting for a father-son acting duo? And so my father and I auditioned. Then calamity struck: I received a green light to be the son of a Blue Lighter, while Dad received no light at all.

Aside from my father's resentment, I had just scheduled my first TV show. I was seventeen years old and earning $5,000 every week. My ego was through the roof; I believed I was the shit, just as everyone else thought Second Chance was. It was ranked 93rd out of the ninety-three shows that season. After the first thirteen episodes, the Saint Peter / Blue Lighter thing was ignored, and the show basically followed myself and my friends on our different excursions. So it didn't matter that the show stayed 93rd on a list of 93rd—someone important had liked me enough to develop a show around me, which just boosted my ego to enormous levels. And it could have set me up for eventual success.

My father reacted with the news by missing every recording except the very last one. I assume he had his reasons.

Valerie was the most attractive woman in the early 1990s. Not only was she lovely and vibrant, but she also had this wonderful, booming, endearing laugh that Craig and I wished to hear all day. Valerie had two new clowns to play with now that Craig and I were cast, and we launched ourselves into those characters with abandon. We had a great time as a group of three.

But being in Sydney and playing the fool with Valerie was more than just amusement for me; it was serious crap. I had to suppress my feelings for her while we worked (this would not be the last time this happened), which was quite difficult. My crush was devastating since she was not only completely out of my league, but she was also married to one of the world's most famous rock artists, Eddie Van Halen. When we were working in Sydney, Eddie's band, Van Halen, was in the midst of four consecutive number one albums—they were perhaps the largest band on the planet in the late 1980s and early 1990s, and Eddie was undoubtedly the greatest rock guitarist on the planet at the time.

It is critical to emphasize that my feelings for Valerie were genuine. I was utterly captivated—I mean, fascinated with her—and fantasized about her leaving Eddie Van Halen and spending the rest of her days with me. I was nineteen years old and lived in a one-bedroom apartment on the corner of Laurel Canyon and Burbank (named Club California, by the way). But fantasies and first loves don't know anything about real estate, or anything else for that matter.

I didn't have a chance in hell. Without a doubt.

That being said, there was one night... I was at Valerie and Eddie's house, just hanging out and trying to make Valerie laugh. You felt ten feet tall when you made her laugh. Eddie had clearly savored the fruits of the vine a little too hard, one more time, and eventually he just went out, not 10 feet away from us, but nevertheless. This was my opportunity! If you think I didn't have a chance in hell, dear reader, you'd be wrong—Valerie and I had a long, intricate make-out session. It was happening—perhaps she was feeling the same way I was. I told her I had been thinking about doing that for a long time, and she agreed. "Heaven" ultimately ended, and I climbed back into my black Honda CRX and drove back to Club California with a hard-on that could have supported the Leaning Tower of Pisa and a nineteen-year-old head saturated with fantasies of a life spent with the object of my affection/obsession.

The next day at work did not go as well as I had hoped. Valerie made no mention of what had occurred and continued to act as if it were simply another day. I soon got the clue and performed the part, but I was crushed on the inside. Many weeping nights and spending most of my daytimes sleeping off hangovers in my tiny trailer—not to mention hours and hours of watching Craig's role as Valerie's love interest grow larger on the show—made for a very miserable disillusioned teenager. The program bombed, and I was relieved that four weeks later, Sydney was canceled, and I wouldn't have to see Valerie again.

But I was nineteen, and life went swiftly for everyone. A year later, Van Halen For Unlawful Carnal Knowledge was released, and I went back to trying to pick up women at the Formosa. And attempting to recreate "the turn" as many times as possible.

It worked occasionally, but every time I left at 1:40 a.m. to hurry to the next liquor store to stock up on vodka and continue drinking late into the night. I'd sit there, emptying the bottle (finally the one with a handle), watching The Goodbye Girl or even Michael Keaton's Clean and Sober (figure that one out), until I passed out, exactly like Eddie Van Halen. A nagging idea had entered my mind as well—not a big one, but one nonetheless: You're drinking every night, though this was swiftly wiped away by the following drink.

And every day, I'd drag myself to lunch, where I'd meet Craig Bierko, who is still by far the fastest comic mind I've ever seen. I thought my thinking was quick, but it was actually Craig Bierko. Hank Azaria became the richest member of the group due to his work as a voice actor on The Simpsons since 1955. I was supposed to be the most famous, while David Pressman was supposed to be a journeyman actor like his father, Laurence Pressman, and the wildest. David liked to go nude into a supermarket and yell, "I have horrible problems, someone please shave me!" before running out. (He did this well into his forties; I occasionally joined him in public disrobing, though I stopped in my mid-thirties because I'm the mature one.)

Aside from attempting to be the quickest and funniest, the other thing that motivated our friendships was fame—we were all desperate to be famous. Hank had the most lucrative job as The Simpsons' voice actor, but it was not the Al Pacino career he desired. As for me, I'd done a lot of TV, but nothing that had even nearly gotten me famous... And all any of us cared about was fame, celebrity, fame. The quieter moments, in between the laughter—and after we'd exchanged the latest stories of auditions gone wrong or scripts we'd read and hated—were filled with a genuine dread, a quiet desire and fear that we would never make it, that stardom would just pass us by. We were four strong egos, four hilarious men, with bon mots shooting around like shrapnel, but the war for fame waged on.

I once had sex with David Pressman, or tried to, though I didn't intend to.

When we were in our early twenties, he and I and a number of other guys headed east to Vegas to do the Vegas thing. We had almost little money, but that had never prevented four morons from coming to Sin City. I suppose I had around $200 in my pocket; the four of us leased a two-bed hotel room off the Strip. I shared a bed with David; I guess I was dreaming about Gaby, my ex, and was inching closer to David in the middle of the night, saying things like "Aw, baby," "You smell so good," and "I promise I'll be quick." He, too, was sound asleep, but his subconscious kept yelling, "NO!" and "back up!" and "leave me the fuck alone!" I eventually started kissing the back of his neck, which startled us both awake; seeing his horrified expression, I murmured, "Aw, just forget it," and scurried back to my side of the bed.

A cab driver drove us out of town to a spot called Dominions, which he assured would satisfy our demands (he likely received a share for every set of naive young guys he dropped off at Dominions in the desert). To even get into this wonderful place, we were told by a man with no neck that we had to pay at least a grand, and as I'd done well at the tables, that honor fell to me. In reality, I ended up spending $1,600 on a single bottle of champagne, after which we were each brought to our own boxy room, where a young lady greeted us.

I believed the $1,600 I'd already paid would be sufficient for whatever came next, but I was tragically mistaken. In fact, I wasn't going to be taken at all unless I offered another $300, which I did, but before I could get to the meat of the event, David Pressman and the other two guys showed up at my door, requiring their own $300 stipend. I returned to the topic at hand after their financial demands were fulfilled. (I didn't think to do the math, but here it is if you need it: I started with $200, won $2,600, spent $1,600 on champagne, and added $300 each for a total of $2,800—everything I had.)

Craig Bierko was the hottest thing in the 1994 pilot season. We were all auditioning for the latest batch of sitcoms and dramas, but Craig was the one everyone wanted. This, and he was faster with a line than I was. He was also far more attractive than me, but let's not get into that—we don't want a sobbing author on our hands. I should have despised him, but since laughter usually triumphs, I decided to keep loving him.

I was twenty-four, and I was already missing half of my auditions. As an actor, I was nearing the end of my career. The fight against auditions was being won slowly but steadily by drinking, and no one was really interested in me anyway. I wasn't getting any movie roles, and the ones I did get on TV weren't exactly ground-breaking. I was hungover half the time and on my way to lunch or the Formosa the rest of the time. One day, my manager sat me down and told me that the individuals I hoped to be—Michael Keaton, Tom Hanks—all exhibited the attitude I was aiming for. But they both looked fantastic, and he was getting daily criticism from casting directors and producers that I was a shambles.

L.A.X. 2194 was a "sci-fi comedy" about Los Angeles International Airport baggage handlers. You could stop there, but there's more: the numerals in the title reveal the twist: it's set two hundred years in the future, and the passengers are aliens. Ryan Stiles would play an automaton office manager with a strange accent (seriously, Ryan is a hilarious actor, but what was that accent?), and I would play the poor guy who had to be the lead in this mess and sort out the baggage issues for the arriving aliens, who happened to be played by Little People in ridiculous wigs.

If all of this sounds underwhelming, remember that it was far worse. For starters, I had to put on a futuristic shirt. Despite my reservations (remember, it was a "comedy" about baggage handlers set two hundred years in the future, with Little People playing the aliens), the pilot paid me $22,500, so I was set for drinks and meals at the Formosa for a while... But it also did something else: because I was linked to L.A.X. 2194, I was no longer available for any other shows.

Then calamity hit, and I don't mean L.A.X. 2194 being picked up for a season—thank God, that didn't happen. What did happen was that a script for a new show called Friends Like Us became the season's most popular read. Everyone who read it knew it was going to be fantastic; when I read it, I immediately called the same agents who had brought me L.A.X. 2194.

It only got worse from there. Because Friends Like Us was the season's hottest ticket, everyone was reading it, auditioning for it, and everyone, it seemed, decided that the role of Chandler was precisely like me and came to my flat to beg me to help them with their auditions. A few even went a long way based solely on my decisions. Hank Azaria believed it was so wonderful that he auditioned for the role of Joey twice. That's right—he auditioned for it, was turned down, begged and pleaded to get back in, and was turned down again. (Later, Hank would be Phoebe's romantic interest for a few episodes, performances for which he received an Emmy. I competed in 237 episodes and won nothing.)

I ended up knowing the screenplay for Friends Like Us by memory because I'd practiced it so much with my friends—there were moments when I just acted Chandler out for them and told them to mimic what I'd done, so I was convinced that it was the right way to play him. Even so, I'd phone my agents every three or four days, pleading for a chance.

My first thought was to tell him to go fuck himself and take his jobs. But because he was a good buddy, Hank and I both agreed. That morning, the three of us read those two scripts, though I already knew Friends Like Us by heart, and it was plain which one he should select. My heart sank because, while I was Chandler, I wasn't an asshole. I was devastated. Craig and I both told him to do Friends Like Us.

I attended the taping of the pilot for Best Friends a few weeks later—it was amusing; Craig was funny, and he got the lead, which is what he really wanted. Perfectly fine, adorable show. However, the final character available during the whole 1994 pilot season, Chandler in Friends Like Us, remained uncast. I was still hooked on the fucking futuristic luggage handler show!

Hello and welcome to my 1994.

NBC producer Jamie Tarses—oh, dear, magical, much-missed Jamie Tarses—who was working on Friends Like Us at NBC—apparently turned to her then-husband, Fox TV producer Dan McDermott, in bed one night.

Marta Kauffman was the person primarily responsible for Friends, along with David Crane. The next day, a Wednesday, I read as Chandler for her, and I broke every rule—for starters, I didn't bring any pages of the screenplay with me (you're meant to take the script with you when you read, because it shows the writers that it's still a work in progress). But at this point, I was so familiar with the script. Of course, I got it right. I read for the production business on Thursday and nailed it, then I read for the network on Friday. You've done it again. I read the words in an unexpected way, emphasizing points that no one else had. I was back in Ottawa with the Murrays, and I was getting laughs where no one else could.

The final actor cast in the 1994 pilot season was Matthew Perry as Chandler Bing.

It was my opiate addiction on overdrive, and I would have loved heroin. I've often compared taking OxyContin to replacing your blood with warm honey. But, with heroin, I'm guessing you're the honey. I enjoyed the sensation of opiates, but the name "heroin" always made me nervous. And it's because of that terror that I'm still alive. There are two types of drug addicts: those who want to get high and those who want to get low. I never understood why the coke guys wanted to feel more present, more occupied. I was a downer; I wanted to melt into my sofa and feel fantastic while watching movies over and over again. I was a calm junkie, not a bull in a china shop.

Sure, without Friends, I could have made a living as a sitcom writer—I'd already written a pilot called Maxwell's House, but despite my abilities, it didn't sell. But I was never going to be a journeyman actor. I wouldn't have kept sober for that; not using heroin was not worth it. Friends was such terrific and fun work that it put a stop to everything for a while. I was the New York Yankees' second baseman. I couldn't mess it up. I'd never forgive myself....

About three weeks before my audition for Friends, I was alone in my Sunset and Doheny tenth-floor apartment—it was modest, but it had a fantastic view, of course—and I was reading about Charlie Sheen in the newspaper. It mentioned Sheen was in trouble again for something, but I remember thinking, "Why does he care—he's famous?"

I got her a ring out of desperation that she would leave me. During Covid, I didn't want to be this injured and alone.

When I asked her to marry me, I was high on 1,800 milligrams of hydrocodone.

I had even sought her family's approval. Then I'd proposed, flying as high as a kite. And down on one knee. And she was well aware of it. And she agreed.

I was in another rehab in Switzerland at the time. This one was in a villa on Lake Geneva with its own butler and chef, the kind of opulent setting where you were guaranteed to be alone. (This effectively defeats the goal of every recovery program I'd ever heard of.) What it lacked in fellow suffering it made up for in easy access to medicines, which sadly did not distinguish it from other high-priced rehabs. If I sued these places, I could win millions, but it would draw more attention to the matter, which I didn't want.

Every day, I also received ketamine infusions. In the 1980s, ketamine was an extremely popular street drug. It is now available in a synthetic form, and it is utilized for two purposes: pain relief and depression relief. It's got my name all over it—they might as well have called it "Matty." Ketamine felt like a massive exhalation. They'd take me into a room, seat me, put headphones on my ears so I could listen to music, blindfold me, and insert an IV. The hardest thing was finding a vein because I'm always a little dehydrated because I don't drink enough water (surprise, surprise). By the end of it, I felt like a fucking pincushion. I was given a smidgeon of Ativan, which I could feel, and then placed on a ketamine drip for an hour. As I lay in the dark listening to Bon Iver, I'd detach, see things—I'd been in therapy for so long that I wasn't even surprised. Is that a horse over there? That's fine—it might as well be.... As the music played and the K passed through me, it all became about the ego and its demise. And I often thought I was going to die during that hour. Oh, this is what happens when you die, I thought. Nonetheless, I kept signing up for this nonsense because it was different, and anything unusual is nice. (This happens to be one of the final lines in Groundhog Day.) Taking K is equivalent to being smacked in the head with a massive happy shovel. However, the hangover exceeded the shovel. Ketamine was not an option for me.

I had a meeting with Adam McKay about a large movie called Don't Look Up right in the middle of all this craziness (but before the rib thing). That day, there was no Chandler—I wasn't on. I couldn't get it up in time for that. We just talked for a few minutes, and as I walked out, I remarked gently, "Well, I'd love to help you in any way I can with this thing."

The next day, I got the call that he was hiring me—this would be the largest movie I'd ever worked on. It promised to be a respite from the storm. I was going to portray a Republican journalist and have three sequences with Meryl Streep. That's correct. I got to do a group scene (with Jonah Hill and others) in Boston, where the movie was shot—I was also on 1,800 mg of hydrocodone at the time, but no one noticed. But I couldn't continue because of the damaged ribs, so I never got to complete my sequences with Meryl. It was painful, but I was in too much pain. God knows how Brees kept throwing the ball, but you don't get to film a scene with Meryl Streep while she has fractured ribs. And I couldn't grin because it ached so much.

Because my life was on fire, being in Don't Look Up didn't work out, but I learnt a crucial lesson: I was hirable in something large without putting on a show. Adam and I were just two males conversing in the meeting. I will cherish that moment, that day, and that man. What a nice person. And I genuinely hope our paths cross again (I'll make sure it's him the next time).

I was still taking 1,800 mg of Oxy every single fucking day when it was time to leave Switzerland. I was promised that whenever I returned to Los Angeles, I'd still be able to collect that much—and I needed it just to keep my head over water. As usual, this was not me getting high; it was strictly maintenance, therefore I didn't suffer. I flew back on a private plane because I couldn't fly commercial because everyone in the world recognized my damn face, and it cost me $175,000 to do so. I returned to Los Angeles to see my doctor.

Back in LA, trying to sober up, I realize, Wait... how did I get engaged? My home is inhabited by dogs. What caused this to happen?

I had approached her parents, pleaded for her hand while high, and endured the dogs. That was how worried I was about being abandoned.

Chapter 4
Like I've Been There Before

It was so special that it felt like we'd all met before or something. Or maybe in another life, but definitely in this one. This was a memorable day. But that was the kind of day that dreams are built of.

For the longest time, I didn't want to talk about Friends too much. Partly because I'd done lots of other things, but everyone always wanted to speak about Chandler—it's like James Taylor talking about "Fire and Rain" (a horrific little yarn if you've ever heard it). It's like a band has written a fantastic new album, but when they perform live, all everybody wants to hear are the hits. I've always respected Kurt Cobain's refusal to perform "Smells Like Teen Spirit," as well as Led Zeppelin's refusal to perform "Stairway to Heaven." According to the New York Times, "Friends... sticks to [Perry] like a sweaty shirt." They weren't wrong—in fact, that's simply fucking cruel—but they weren't the only ones who thought so. I was really good at something, but I was getting punished for it. Every Friday night, I left my blood, sweat, and tears onstage—we all did. And that should be a positive thing, not something that implies we can only excel at one thing.

I was the last actor cast in the entire 1994 pilot season—in fact, I received the job on the final day of the season.

With L.A.X. 2194 mercifully behind me, I was free to be Chandler Bing. The Monday after the Friday I was hired was day one of my new life—this was important, and I think we all sensed it because we all showed up on time. Matt LeBlanc was first every day, and Aniston was last every day. The cars improved, but the order remained unchanged.

We became buddies a few years later, ironically. Fortunately, even though I was still attracted to her and thought she was fantastic, we were able to sail right past the past on that first day and focus on the fact that we had both received the best job Hollywood has to offer.

Courteney Cox was staggeringly lovely in a yellow gown. Lisa Kudrow had been recommended to me by a mutual acquaintance, and she was just as beautiful, witty, and highly smart as my friend had described. David Schwimmer had had his hair cut pretty short (he had been portraying Pontius Pilate for his theater ensemble in Chicago) over his hangdog face and was incredibly entertaining right immediately; kind, witty, and inventive. He was the one who pitched the most jokes after me—I probably pitched 10 jokes a day and only two of them got in. They weren't just for me; I'd pitch them to everyone. "You know, it might be funny if you tried to say this..." I'd say to Lisa, and she'd try it.

I'd always wanted to be the only one who laughed. But now, at the age of twenty-four, I've understood that it's preferable if everyone is amusing. I could tell this was going to be enormous right away; I knew it from the start, but I didn't say anything. Part of this was due to the fact that it is not uncommon for an actor to screw up a table read so terribly that they were politely asked to leave before a single minute of shooting occurred. But that would have to wait until tomorrow; for now, Jimmy had taken the six of us to Monica's apartment set and ordered us to just talk to one another. So we talked and laughed about romance, our careers, our loves, and our losses. And the bond Jimmy had predicted would be crucial has begun.

Given her status—she'd appeared on Family Ties, Ace Ventura, Seinfeld, and had danced with Bruce Springsteen in the video for

"Dancing in the Dark"—she could have been everything and everyone; she might easily have said, "I'm the star." She could have had her lunch someplace else and we'd have been cool with it. Instead, she simply stated, "Let's really work together and get to know each other." She stated it was what she'd noticed about how it worked on Seinfeld, and she hoped it would hold true for Friends as well.

The second day was crucial. For our first table read, we went to a new facility, facility 40. I was nervous, excited, and confident all at the same time. Table reads have always come naturally to me. But there was still the lurking possibility that anyone could be dismissed and replaced (for example, Lisa Kudrow was originally cast as Roz on Frasier but was sacked during the rehearsal process by none other than... Friends director, Jimmy Burrows). If jokes didn't land or something was amiss, anyone might be replaced before they'd even made it to their dressing room.

But I recognized Chandler. Chandler and I could shake hands. I pretended to be him.

The place was full that day, with standing room only. There were writers, executives, and network personnel present. There must have been a hundred people in the room, but I was a song-and-dance guy, and this was my forte. We reconnected with Marta Kauffman, David Crane, and Kevin Bright—the creators behind the show and who had recruited us—and we all felt like they were our parents almost immediately.

This show was going to be successful, and it was going to transform everyone's life for the better. I swear I heard a popping sound; if you listened closely, you could hear it. It was the sound of people's wishes being granted.

It was all I had hoped for. Friends Like Us was intended to fill in all the gaps. Charlie Sheen is a jerk. I was going to be so renowned that all the grief I was carrying would melt away like frost in the sun, and any new threats would bounce off me as if this show were a force field I could cloak myself in.

I drove home on a cloud that evening. There was no traffic; all of the traffic signals were green; and a drive that should have lasted half an hour took fifteen minutes. The attention that I had always felt eluded me was going to flood every part of my existence, like a burst of lightning. People were starting to like me. I was going to be sufficient. I was important. I wasn't overly needy. I was a celebrity.

We practiced for the rest of the week, and it was then that we noticed something else. That had never happened to me as an actor before or since, and it was beautiful: the employers were not in the least tyrannical. In reality, it was a very creative environment. We could pitch jokes, and the best one would win, regardless of where it originated from. What did the craft services lady say that was amusing? It didn't matter where you put it. So I was there not only as an actor, but also as a creative force.

This was all too true for both Chandler and me. I knew early on in the production of Friends that I still had a huge crush on Jennifer Aniston. Our greetings and farewells were awkward. And then I'd wonder, "How long can I look at her?" Is three seconds excessive?

And I was speaking in a way that no one had ever spoken in a sitcom before, hitting weird emphases, picking a word in a sentence that you would not think was the beat, employing the Murray-Perry Cadence. I didn't realize it at the time, but my way of speaking would permeate the society over the next few decades—for now, I was just trying to find fascinating ways into phrases that were already humorous, but that I believed I could genuinely make dance. (Marta Kauffman subsequently said that the writers would underline the word that wasn't generally emphasized in a sentence just to see what I'd do with it.)

I realized the script was unique when I first read it because it was so character-driven and intelligent. But Matt LeBlanc was worried early on that because he was portrayed as a suave, macho ladies' man in the script, Rachel, Monica, and Phoebe wouldn't be friends with him, wouldn't like him all that much, making his role less believable.

Matt would come into my dressing room on occasion, mostly during season one, and ask me how to say his lines. And I'd tell him, and he'd walk downstairs, and he'd nail it... However, he received the Most Improved Player because, by season ten, I was going into his room and asking him how he would pronounce certain of my lines.

This was only the beginning. For the time being, we were filming shows in preparation for our fall 1994 air date. And no one knew who we were yet.

With the shows completed, all that remained was to determine our time slot. NBC felt they had something unique on their hands, so they sandwiched us between Mad About You and Seinfeld. It was the ideal location; plum. Because this was before streaming, your time slot was critical. It was still the days of appointment television, when people would rush home to see the 8:00 or 9:00 p.m. show. And people planned their life around their shows rather than the other way around. So 8:30 p.m. on a Thursday between two enormous performances was a tremendous deal.

We took the Warner Bros. aircraft to New York for the "upfronts." The upfronts are the presentations of a show to the affiliates. On this trip, they informed us that the show's name had been changed to Friends (when they renamed it, I thought it was a terrible idea—I never said I was a smart person), and Friends was a smash with the affiliates as well—everything was falling into place. We were celebrating, getting drunk, and partying in New York before heading to Chicago for more upfronts and partying.

When I met Gwyneth, I was back in Williamstown, Massachusetts. She was there for a play, and I was there to see my grandfather. We went into a broom cupboard and made out at a big party. We were both still unknown enough that it didn't make it into the headlines, so it was up to Jimmy Burrows to give me a reality check.

I still desired fame, but I could detect a strange flavor in the air— would fame, that elusive lover, truly fill all the gaps I carried about with me? What if I couldn't put twenty on black in a dimly lit casino with a vodka tonic in my hand without someone shouting, "Matthew

Perry just put twenty on black, everyone, come and see!" This was the final summer of my life when I could make out with a gorgeous young woman named Gwyneth at a party and no one cared except Gwyneth and I.

Would I ever be able to replicate anonymously my twenty-first birthday, when I'd drunk seven 7 and 7s, poured a bottle of wine into a huge brandy snifter—you know, the one they put on the piano for tips—ordered a cab, gotten into the back of the cab with the snifter, still sipping the wine, tried to give directions to my home when I could only pronounce the letter L, only for the guy up front to

I flew to Mexico by myself late in the summer of 1994. I'd recently split up with Gaby and decided to go on a booze cruise by myself. I strolled around Cabo, getting drunk and calling girls in LA from my room. Then, every night on the trip, I'd go to some strange party where everyone was frightened until they handed out a jug of booze, at which point it was all over. I was lonely, I hadn't gotten laid, and it was hot in Cabo but frigid inside me. I could feel God watching and waiting for me. The most terrifying thing was that I thought God was omniscient, which meant he already knew what he had in store for me.

We weren't about to leave. We were the epitome of prime time, back when prime time still mattered. The television gold rush. Even more crucial than the positive reviews was the fact that we had only lost around 20% of the crowd for Mad around You, which was an exceptionally strong result for a new production. We were beating Mad About You by episode six, indicating that we were a tremendous hit. We quickly rose to the top ten, then the top five, and we would remain there for the next decade. This is still unheard of.

I flew to New York in late October 1995, between the airings of episodes five and six of season two, to make my first appearance on the Late Show, when being on Letterman was the pinnacle of pop culture celebrity. I was dressed in a black suit, and Letterman would point to my lapel and say, "late 1960s, British Invasion, kinda mod."

Everything was in order. Everything was perfect. I had just turned twenty-five years old. I was in the world's largest sitcom; I was in a hotel in New York, watching as world leaders were rushed into elevators by security forces, putting on a thousand-dollar suit before joshing it up with Dave Letterman.

This was a celebrity. And God peered down on me, just beyond the glare of the city, past the skyscrapers and the faint stars sparkling beyond the midtown skies. He has all of the time in the world. He invented time, fuck.

Best Friends, the show he preferred above Friends Like Us, had fizzled. (Later, Warren Littlefield, former NBC network president, wrote in his memoir about Craig's decision not to choose Friends, "Thank God! Craig Bierko had a Snidely Whiplash vibe to him. He appeared to be filled with rage underneath. It's difficult to find a beautiful leading man who is also funny.") He was working steadily—he'd later feature in The Music Man on Broadway and The Long Kiss Goodnight with Geena Davis and Sam Jackson, among other things—but our fortunes had diverged, and our friendship was on fire.

I was missing him. He was still the most quick-witted humorous mind I'd ever met, which I admired. I couldn't go to the Formosa just to hang out; I missed that life as well. I'd started drinking alone in my flat since it was the safest option. The disease was worsening, but I couldn't see it. If anyone saw how much I was drinking, they could become concerned and ask me to stop. And, of course, stopping was impossible.

Craig Bierko, on the other hand, called me out of the blue one day. He wanted to pay me a visit. I was both happy and concerned. You know how it feels when you wind up dating someone who had a crush on your best friend? It felt like that; I'd assumed the role he could and should have taken, and everything had gone gold for me, then platinum, then some other undiscovered precious metal.

I'd give everything to not feel this way. It's not just a passing idea for me; it's a coldhearted fact. That Faustian prayer I prayed was silly, like a child's prayer. It had nothing to do with reality.

Chapter 5
No Fourth Wall

Taos, New Mexico, New Year's Eve 1995. We'd been playing football in the snow all afternoon. Julia Roberts, my girlfriend, and a slew of our pals. She was the biggest movie star in the world, and I was on the most popular television show.

Initially, the wooing was done via fax. A two-foot-long courtship, full with poems and flights of imagination and two gigantic stars falling for each other and uniting in a lovely, romantic way, exists somewhere in the globe.

Friends' first season had been a big hit, and I had practically drifted into season two. I'd done Letterman and was scheduled to do Leno. We'd graced the covers of People and Rolling Stone magazines when both were huge. Now the film offers were pouring in. Why wouldn't they? I was receiving whatever I wanted. A million-dollar film offer here, a million-dollar film offer there. I wasn't Julia Roberts, but there were only a few of us.

Then something only celebrities experience occurred. Marta Kauffman contacted me and suggested that I deliver flowers to Julia Roberts.

Do you mean the universe's biggest star, Julia Roberts?

Julia had been offered the post-Super Bowl episode in season two, but she would only do the program if she could be a part of my plot line. Let me state it again: she would only do the program if she could be a part of my plot. (Was I having a good or bad year?) But first, I needed to entice her.

The next day, I emailed her a paper about wave-particle duality, the uncertainty principle, and entanglement, only some of which was metaphorical. Many years later, Alexa Junge, a staff writer on the program, told The Hollywood Reporter, "[Julia] was interested in [Matthew] from afar because he's so charming." There was a lot of flirtation going on around faxing. She was filling out questionnaires for him, such as, 'Why should I go out with you?' And everyone in the writers' room pitched in to help him explain why. He could get by without us, but there was no doubt we were on Team Matthew and working hard to make it happen for him."

All of our efforts paid off in the end. Julia not only agreed to go on the show, but she also sent me a gift: bagels—many and lots of bagels. Yes, why not? Julia Roberts was there.

Thus began a three-month fax-based courtship. This was pre-internet, pre-cell phones, and all of our communication was done via fax. And there were hundreds of them. At first, it was on the outside of romance: I sent her poems, asked her to identify the Los Angeles Kings' triple title line, and so on. And it's not like we weren't both busy—I was filming the most popular program on the globe, and she was in France filming a Woody Allen film, Everyone Says I Love You. (She was, of course.) But three or four times a day, I'd sit by my fax machine, watching the piece of paper gently unfold to show her next missive. I was so pleased that some evenings I'd find myself at a party, having a flirting chat with a beautiful woman, and then cutting the conversation short so I could run home and see if a new fax had arrived. One had nine times out of 10. They were so clever—the way she wove sentences together, the way she saw the world, the way she conveyed her own thoughts. It wasn't uncommon for me to read these faxes three, four, or even five times while smirking at the paper like a lunatic. It seemed as if she had been sent to this planet to make everyone happy, including me. I was giddy as a fifteen-year-old on his first date.

I grabbed the phone and dialed Julia Roberts' number. I was as nervous as I had been since my first appearance on Letterman. But the talk was easy—I made her laugh, and what a laugh it was.... She was obviously incredibly intelligent. I could tell right away that she was easily in the top three storytellers I'd ever met. Her anecdotes were so brilliant, in fact, that I asked her whether she had planned them ahead of time.

As we drew to a conclusion after five and a half hours, I realized I wasn't nervous any longer. We couldn't stop talking after that—five-hour chats here, four-hour conversations there. We were falling; I wasn't sure where we were falling, but we were falling.

But it was New Year's Eve in Taos when we shot it. It was the year 1996. Julia Roberts was my girlfriend. I'd even met her parents. She drove me there in her orange Volkswagen Beetle after I had flown there privately. I assumed I had money. She was wealthy.

We climbed a mountain in this large blue vehicle, snow swirling around us. I didn't know where we were headed. We appeared to be ascending into the very stars themselves. We eventually arrived at a peak, where the clouds parted and we could see New Mexico and beyond, all the way back to Canada. She made me feel like the ruler of the world as we sat there. The year 1996 began with a moderate snowfall.

Julia appeared on Letterman in February, and he grilled her on whether or not we were dating. She has recently appeared as a guest star in the Friends episode "The One After the Super Bowl." That program, which featured guest performers such as Julia, Jean-Claude Van Damme, Brooke Shields, and Chris Isaak, among others, was watched by 52.9 million people, making it the most watched show ever to follow a Super Bowl. The ad income alone was staggering—more than $500,000 for thirty seconds of television. The show was now firmly established as NBC's main cash cow.

Julia's segment of the double episode was shot a few days after New Year's, from January 6 to 8. "Back then, I used humor as a defense mechanism—thank God I don't do that anymore," they'd wrote, adding "I've met the perfect woman." Our couch kiss was so lifelike that everyone assumed it was real.

On film, not only is the process slower, but it also only works if you truly feel what you're attempting to depict as a feeling. This deeper work can be tough to transfer to, and I found it especially difficult because sequences in movies are often shot out of order.

On day two of Fools Rush In, we were filming a scene at the obstetrician's office, and I recall hearing our baby's heartbeat for the first time. Given that I'd only recently met Salma, I had no idea how to acquire a feel for it. Later on, I recall a situation that made me want to cry. That made me nervous as well. I had been thinking about it all day and worried about it all night. I managed to pull it off somehow. The approach is simple: think of anything that makes you sad. However, timing is tricky because you must perform it at precisely the proper time and over and over again.

I went over the script and pitched gags to Andy Tennant, who was a really smart and extremely pleasant person, during the film's production. He sat on me—I was hopping around doing my silly little things—and he'd pull me aside and say, "You don't have to do that." You're intriguing enough to keep an eye on without doing that."

Then I turned the Jet Ski sharply right, while my body continued straight ahead. I was in the air, and then I wasn't. When I surfaced, I looked back to where I'd begun, and there stood forty people on the shoreline, the entire crew, who had been watching me risk my life throughout the film, and who had now all jumped into Lake Mead to retrieve me.

I knew I was harmed when I got back to shore. That night, there was a big scene to shoot—the delivery of the kid, the pivotal moment—and I had to be there. But everything hurt, and I had really messed up my neck. The crew recognized my distress and summoned a doctor, who stopped by my trailer and delivered me a single medication in a plastic container.

In Fools Rush In, my character is a real estate entrepreneur who drives a red Mustang. The action lasted all night, but we finished just before daybreak. The sun was getting closer to the horizon.

When I left the parking lot, the first light of the Nevada day was seeping over Mount Wilson. I lowered the top of that Mustang and consumed the pill. I thought of Julia; I imagined myself flying above Lake Mead, carefree. I reflected on my childhood, but it didn't bother me at the time. Something clicked in me when the drug kicked in. And it's been that click that I've been looking for for the rest of my life. I reflected on Craig Bierko, the Murray brothers, and Friends. Summer was approaching, with its pink cirrus clouds and gentle, arid air. My pink sky looked like this. If a locomotive struck me, I would just turn to the engineer and remark, "It happens, brother." I was lying in the grass in my backyard in Canada, surrounded once more by Murray puke. I couldn't believe how great I felt; I was completely and utterly euphoric. The medication had replaced my blood with warm honey in my body. I felt like I was on top of the world. It was the most amazing sensation I'd ever felt. Nothing could possibly go wrong. I recall thinking as I drove that red Mustang convertible to my leased house in Vegas, "If this doesn't kill me, I'm doing it again." Of course, this is a negative memory because of what happened after, but it was also a good memory. That morning, I felt near to God. I had experienced heaven, something not many people do. That morning, I shook God's hand.

Be cautious, Matty; something that feels so pleasant must have consequences. I'm aware of the implications now, and boy, am I aware of them. But I didn't know them at the time. I wish that was the end of my thoughts on Fools Rush In. Fun insider anecdotes on how movies are made. I hate to bust the celebrity-industrial complex bubble, but there are real people behind the glitter and martini shots and A-cameras. What no one could see was that someone's life, most likely the least probable candidate, was about to plunge through the gates of hell.

After a year and a half, I was taking 55 of those medications every day. My life was in shambles when I entered Hazelden recovery in Minnesota, weighing 128 pounds. I was terrified, convinced I was going to die, and had no idea what had happened to me. I wasn't looking to die; I just wanted to feel better.

Of course, the fact that "Matthew Perry is in rehab" became a major news issue. I wasn't even given the chance to hash out my difficulties in private. Everyone was aware. It was on the covers of every magazine—I didn't even have the obscurity that everyone else did. I was scared. I was also young, so I recovered quickly. I was back on my feet and looking healthy in twenty-eight days.

Making movies is a very different beast than making television. If you were sad about something on Friends, you'd play it up as if you were the saddest person in the world—basically, for the back row of the live audience. Your performance also has a wink to the audience, as if to say, "Hey, everybody, watch this." You're going to love it." Every week on a sitcom, it's like performing a one-act play. There are 300 individuals in the crowd, and you must open up to them.

On Friends, everyone had their own years when the entire world was talking about their character. Season one was David Schwimmer's; season two was Lisa; seasons five and six were Courteney and myself; Jen was seasons seven and eight, and Matt (Most Improved Friend) was seasons nine and ten. Some of them won Emmys for those seasons, and I believe all of us should have won more, but I believe there is a bias against gorgeous rich people with apartments that are far too large for reality in New York City... Except, as I was continuously saying, there was no fourth wall.

David showed up one day in my dressing room during that first year. He'd given his persona a unique hangdog expression, and he was hilarious. He was also the first of us to shoot a commercial, appear on The Tonight Show, buy a property, and star in his own film. That first year, he was undeniably the hot man. He'd been amusing.

Being on Friends was one of those once-in-a-lifetime experiences in which the news just kept getting better and better. But things weren't going so smoothly off-screen. I went on Jay Leno in late April 1996 and confessed I was single. It had been too much for me to date Julia Roberts. I was convinced she was going to end her relationship with me—why wouldn't she? I was insufficient; I could never be sufficient; I was broken, bent, and unlovable. So, rather than go through the misery of losing her, I ended my relationship with the stunning and great Julia Roberts. She might have thought she was slumming it with a TV person, and now the TV guy was breaking up with her. I can't even begin to explain her puzzled expression.

I opted to party with the Murray brothers on Cape Cod. I'm not sure why I chose Cape Cod or why the Murray brothers joined me. I assumed it was just a new bar to try out. But it was then that I recognized something had changed—a new dynamic was at work. The days of anxiously approaching ladies with poor lines were past; girls were approaching me and talking to me. They approached me as I stood in a corner with a vodka tonic in my hand.

But none of them were Julia Roberts.

I've detoxed over 65 times in my life, the first time when I was twenty-six.

My Vicodin habit had now become really problematic. If you watch Friends season three, I hope you're shocked at how thin I am at the end of the season (opioids mess with your appetite and make you puke all the time). In the last episode, you'll see that I'm wearing a white shirt and tan slacks, both of which appear to be at least three sizes too large for me. (Compare this to how I perceive the final episode of season six and the first episode of season seven—the Chandler-Monica proposal episodes. I'm wearing the same clothing in the sixth and seventh episodes [which are intended to air on the same night], but I must have lost fifty pounds in the off-season. During Friends years, my weight fluctuated between 128 and 225 pounds.)

You can follow the progression of my addiction by comparing my weight from season to season—when I'm overweight, it's drink; when I'm thin, it's medicine. I take a lot of medicines when I have a goatee.

By the end of season three, I was spending the majority of my time finding out how to get fifty-five Vicodin each day—I had to have fifty-five every day or I'd become sick. Making calls, seeing doctors, faking migraines, and locating corrupt nurses who would give me what I needed was a full-time job.

I swiftly booked another film, Almost Heroes, a comedy directed by Christopher Guest and starring Chris Farley. For that, they paid me

$2 million. We shot it in a slum area of Northern California, near Eureka. Farley was as amusing as you'd expect, though his addictions, along with mine, meant that we barely made it through the stupid thing. I was exhausted from shooting Friends and Almost Heroes at the same time. The medicines weren't working as they used to. To avoid feeling sick all the time, I had to take a particular quantity of pills.

Eating also interfered with the high, so I never ate. In addition, I was always so nauseous that I didn't want to eat. I couldn't stop vomiting. This was good in private, but not so much in the middle of the woods with Christopher Guest. You're going to puke in thirty seconds. You'd better find a way to excuse yourself quickly. I puked behind trees, behind rocks, and in ladies' restrooms. I'd heard of individuals rummaging through their own vomit for pill bits to re-administer, but I couldn't bring myself to do it. I already had so many doctors on staff that I was rarely in that situation. But I did keep two towels by my toilet, one to wipe away the vomit and the other to wipe away the tears. I knew I was dying, but I couldn't tell anyone.

Then Chris Farley passed away. His sickness had advanced faster than mine. (Plus, I had a healthy horror of the word "heroin," which neither of us shared.) When I found out, I punched a hole in Jennifer Aniston's dressing room wall. Keanu Reeves is amongst us. I had to promote Almost Heroes two weeks after he died, and I found myself publicly describing his drug and alcohol-related death.

The goal was for me to go through a quick detox before heading up to Minnesota. In a fast detox, you are sedated for two or three days and are given opiate antagonists. You're expected to be sober by the end of it. (By the way, I now know it doesn't work, despite the fact that it's still used as a treatment.)

So I completed the quick detox and then headed up to Hazelden, but when I got there, I felt like I was dying. They say that opioid detoxes can't kill you, but they can make you wish you were dead. (Alcohol and benzos are the detoxes that can kill you.) I was in my Hazelden room, and I was extremely sick—I kicked like a fucking dog. Legs and arms quivering and jerking in dread. I was constantly pleading for help, only to be told, "You're detoxed, just relax."

But I hadn't detoxed—I'd simply gone from 55 Vicodins per day to zero Vicodins per day, effectively cold turkey. I became a "wall hugger"—to take even a few feet, I had to grasp onto the nearest wall.

I know now that if I hadn't done the rapid detox, I would have been given something to relieve the pain, but they assumed I'd detoxed and left me alone. I suppose going from fifty-five to nothing indicates I was a fucking strong person, but it was the purest kind of agony.

The year leading up to Hazelden had been the best year of my life, the best year anyone could dream for. If I'd died then, my headstone would have read either: HERE LIES MATTHEW PERRY—HE BROKE UP WITH JULIA ROBERTS or, COULD I BE MORE STUPID AND DEAD?

I fell hard for a woman I was working with on a film in 1999. (I was beginning to develop a pattern of falling for famous ladies, just as my mother had in Canada.) All the barriers had come down, and I was simply me... She then chose someone else to fall in love with.

I've gotten most of the people I've desired, yet this one still hurts. Which just goes to show that the exception proves the rule: when I can have someone, I have to leave them before they leave me, because I'm not enough and I'm about to be discovered, but when someone I want doesn't choose me, it just goes to show that I'm not enough and I've been discovered. They win with heads, and I lose with tails. In any case, whenever her name is spoken, my gut clenches. The nightmare that had consumed my every waking thought had come true. She had even indicated that my drinking was a problem, which was yet another cost of my addiction. You'd think that would help someone get sober, but it actually made things worse. I placed candles all throughout my house, drank, and watched the movie we were watching together, tormenting myself, alone, heartbroken, and attempting to move on. Failing.

Me? I couldn't leave my room since I was taking so many medicines. So, at a time when Matthew Perry should have been rejoicing and being the top of the town, I was dealing with drug dealers and living in dark rooms and despair.

But the addiction still plagued me—once, in a scene in the café while dressed in a suit, I fell asleep right on the couch, and tragedy was averted only when Matt LeBlanc prodded me awake immediately before my line; no one noticed, but I knew how close I'd come.

Then I had pancreatitis. I was thirty years old at the time.

It was during the break. I was alone once more, and nothing was happening—no movie to film, nothing, just slow, tar-like time seeping down the LA canyons toward the unending sea. I was basically staying at home for months drinking—alone so I could drink; alone because I was drinking. (As I have stated, alcoholism is frantic to get you out on your own.) I was watching Meet Joe Black on repeat, despite the fact that it's about the character Death (me) attempting to discover what love is. Perfect. But it was as if I were Joe Black, being asked again and over, "What do we do now?" I was like death—I'd drink, watch the movie, pass out, wake up, drink, watch the movie again, and pass out again.

I was in the hospital for thirty days and nights, being fed fluids through an IV (the only way to treat pancreatitis was to leave the pancreas completely alone, which meant I couldn't eat or drink anything for about thirty days); and every one of those nights, I'd fall asleep with Jamie Tarses by my side—she had a bed moved in, the whole shebang—and I'd wake up to find her there, too. (I still feel Jamie was a kind God's emissary, and that none of us were worthy of her—I certainly wasn't.) While I smoked in my hospital room, we'd watch The West Wing over and over. It was either a different era or I was so famous at the time that it didn't matter. At one point, they apprehended me and instructed me to halt. But since I was desperate, I checked myself out of the hospital, smoked, and then checked myself back in.

They hooked me up to a machine that gave me regular doses of a pain reliever called Dilaudid. If only it arrived in human form, it is an opioid that modifies the brain's connection to pain. But Dilaudid was my new favorite medicine, and I could have stayed in that hospital for a hundred days if they had kept giving it to me. I had Jamie by my side for thirty days, and I was high and joyful. I was very thrilled when I signed the deal for seasons six and seven, which brought us $50 million thanks to David Schwimmer's unselfish and great initiative. With a feeding tube in my arm and Dilaudid coursing through my veins, I signed the contract.

It was an acceptable choice, and as I had nothing better to do, I returned to my home on Chelan Way in the Hollywood Hills to pick up some items. I was sober, but I'd only been on Dilaudid for thirty days, so I was still a little loopy. Jamie waited while I packed a bag, and then I followed her in my green Porsche out through the Hills' winding roads. As I turned left onto Chelan Drive, there was a courier van coming straight at me, so I swerved and pumped the brakes, but the car hit some grass and just kept going, and I drove into the stairs leading up to a house, demolishing them, and then into the living room. Fortunately, no one was home, but the car and stairs were totaled.

It seemed like I was fifteen again, living in California with my father. Every day, a car would arrive to pick me up and drive me to the Friends set. But it wasn't long before I picked up Vicodin again, and then I started drinking and liked it again. "Reality is an acquired taste," my therapist said, and I had failed to acquire it. I was sneaking drugs and alcohol into my father's house, and his wife was so upset that my father approached me gently and informed me that I had to leave.

I'd already heard about methadone, a medicine that claimed to be able to kick a fifty-five-a-day Vicodin addict in one day with just one sip. The only catch was that you had to drink that little taste every day or go into severe withdrawal. My frantic mind thought, "Sounds good to me." I took the medicine right away and was ready to go back to Friends the next day.

When I wasn't feeling well enough to drive to the set (I never worked high, but I certainly worked hungover), I'd hire a limo—that will get you some strange stares, let me tell you. Everyone would ask if I was okay, but no one wanted to stop the Friends train since it was so profitable, and I felt terrible about it. My greatest joy was also my greatest fear—I was so close to ruining this lovely thing.

I eventually found a sober coworker, but it wasn't really helpful. I had taken some kind of drug and had drunk the night before, and it all came together during a run-through in front of everyone one day. But there was a strange twist to this one: I was hammered but didn't realize it, so I assumed I had nothing to hide. I had no idea I was drunk, yet I was slurring. People couldn't understand a single word I said. However, I had no idea.

Serving Sara was a lousy film, but it was made even worse by my performance in it.

I was in bad shape and had overextended myself. I was working on the film four days a week and then going back to Los Angeles on a private plane to do Friends. I'd have a water bottle filled with vodka on the plane that I'd sip from as I went over my lines. (In fact, if you're keeping track, I was on methadone, Xanax, cocaine, and a full quart of vodka every day.) When I arrived in Dallas for a scene, I realized we'd already shot it a few days before. Things were starting to fall apart.

Jamie Tarses—beautiful, lovely, kind, and brilliant. Jamie Tarses traveled out to Texas to be my nurse, but I was still drinking and taking drugs and trying to keep it all a secret from her. We were watching TV one night when she turned to me and said, "It looks like you're disappearing."

I put down the book and began to cry. I'm crying just thinking about it. I wasn't the only one. There were a large number of folks who shared my viewpoint. (This line was penned by William Silkworth on July 27, 1938.) It was an incredible and terrifying moment all at the same time. This statement indicated that I will never be alone again. It also meant that I was an alcoholic who would have to stop drinking and drugging right now and every day for the rest of my life, one day at a time.

"This guy is hard-core," Marina del Rey residents claimed. Thirty days will not suffice for him. He needs long-term care." So they transferred me to a Malibu recovery facility, where I spent the first twelve days not sleeping at all. My liver enzymes were skyrocketing. But after approximately three months, I began to improve—I participated in the groups and "did the work," as they say.

When Monica and Chandler married, I was in recovery. It was the 17th of May, 2001.

I'd been detoxing for two months when the powers that be decided to give us all the night off to watch the Academy Awards on March 25, 2001. I was lying there, sweaty and twitching, terrified and barely paying attention, when Kevin Spacey went up to the podium and said:

"And the Oscar goes to … Julia Roberts!"

I watched as Julia kissed her then-boyfriend, actor Benjamin Bratt, and proceeded up the steps to accept her award.

I climbed into bed and stared at the ceiling on Julia's big night in Hollywood. That night, I wouldn't be able to sleep. Just thoughts flying through my head like a bullet discharged into a tin can. That blue truck, and that mountain peak. All the blue vehicles, all the mountaintops, disappeared like ether in a terror vacuum. I was quite thrilled for her. As for me, I was simply grateful to have survived another day. The days are long when you're at the bottom.

I didn't need an Oscar; all I wanted was one more day.

Addiction is similar to the Joker. It only wants to see the entire world burn.

Chapter 6
All Heaven Breaking Loose

I was feeling better after three months of therapy.

I was really happy to be back on my feet and live a life that was not completely dictated by my booze and addiction. I had stopped drinking and doing drugs. And my desire for each had vanished. Something much, much bigger than me was suddenly in charge. Miracles do occur.

After all of that, it's astounding how many ladies joined up for this. Many of them, I'm sure, thought they could change me. What do you mean? Of course, there was the occasional abrupt walkout. A few ladies would remark, "Well, I'm not interested in that at all," and walk away. (It's no surprise that those were the ones I was most interested in.)

I use the term "worked" quite loosely. Because it goes without saying that the best you could say about all of this is that you could swap my head for a donkey's ass and no one would notice. Not only had I just broken up with the most beautiful lady on the planet, but what I was proposing was a complete waste of time. Sex is fine and all, but I believe I would be a much happier person now if I had spent those years looking for anything more.

This may have been my biggest blunder in a life full of them. And mistakes are difficult to reverse.

During that time, I met at least five ladies with whom I could have married and raised children. If I'd only done it once, I wouldn't be sitting in a huge house overlooking the beach with no one to share it with except a sober friend, a nurse, and a gardener twice a week—a gardener I'd frequently go outside and give a hundred dollars to so he'd turn off his fucking leaf blower. (How come we can send a man on the moon but not create a silent one?)

One of these women was Natasha Wagner. She's not only gorgeous, brilliant, kind, and sensual; she's also the daughter of Natalie Wood and Richard Gregson (and was raised by Robert Wagner and Jill St. John after her mother's terrible death). Natasha had everything; she was flawless! But I wasn't aiming for perfection; I wanted more. Much more, much more. So, because I'd given her the speech and then failed to date her properly, we split up, and I was left to find even more beautiful women when I'd already found them.

A few years later, I was driving down the Pacific Coast Highway in some type of fuck-off-everyone automobile, a car so fantastic that I can't remember what make it was. The top was down, and the gleaming sun was plucking at the edges of the surf out in the water, turning it into a slippery silver. Dudes on surfboards sat around waiting for The One, who never arrived; I knew precisely how they felt.

My phone then rang. Natasha was the one. She'd fallen for me after one of these dates, so she'd had to leave—that's the rule, Matty, that's the rule!—but she was still a friend, even if I'd dumped her.

Maybe if she called, there was a chance we could...?

"I'm a mother!" she said. "I recently gave birth to a baby girl." Clover!"

"Oh...," I said, then soon recovered, or so I thought. "That's wonderful news, honey. "I adore that name as well!"

"She could have had that child with me," I told no one, sobbing like a baby.

It was up to me to figure out why I'd broken down so badly. I sat there, thinking and wondering, until I realized what I'd been doing: I'd been hunting for an hour or two of pleasure with every woman ever invented when there was so much life I was missing. Is this why I became sober? To have sex with women? Surely, God had something greater in mind for me.

I'd have to find out quickly. Natasha's life was flowering, whilst mine was spiraling out of control.

I was dating everyone and anybody in LA, but I'd found a woman I genuinely adored in New York. I wasn't faithful to her, but I loved her anyway. I was newly sober and renowned, and I wanted to fuck everyone in Los Angeles County; many agreed. My speech was far more effective than it had any right to be. But the woman I fell in love with in New York was like a nice mother—a fantastic caretaker and so gorgeous that of course I was drawn to her and, of course, I messed it up. But it wasn't all bad—in LA, I was also working to assist other alcoholics become sober—sponsoring individuals, answering phone calls when necessary, and giving counsel. Friends was also a juggernaut, and I didn't have to worry about screwing that up because I was clean and ready to have my season, the one where everyone was talking about Chandler. (I was fully sober for the entire Friends season in 1989. Do you want to guess which year I was nominated for an Emmy for outstanding actor in a comedy? Season nine, indeed. Nothing will tell you anything if that doesn't. What was it that I did differently that season? I paid attention. I didn't simply stand there waiting for my turn to speak. Listening is sometimes more powerful than speaking. I've attempted to incorporate it into my daily life as well. Learn more and talk less. That has been my new slogan.)

In 1999, I was sitting alone in my way-too-large mansion at the top of Carla Ridge, yet another house with a stunning view of the Los Angeles Basin. Normal Los Angeles life was going on someplace down there (Tar Pits; Walk of Fame)—up here, I was just waiting it out—drink in one hand, a continuous flow of Marlboro Lights in the other. Friends was five seasons in; Ross and Rachel had just stumbled out of a church wedded, ahead of Chandler and Monica. Friends was a cultural landmark, a millennium's shorthand, the world's number one show, and everyone's favorite show to watch.

A messenger had arrived at my door, breaking my meditation. It was as if I were reenacting what had happened to the Romantic poet Coleridge, who had been interrupted from his own high—he got his from opium—by the fabled "person from Porlock." Coleridge had memorized the entirety of his poem "Kubla Khan" at the time, but the messenger who had arrived at his door that day in 1797 had broken that memory, leaving only fifty-four lines for posterity.

I wasn't Coleridge, but the view and the vodka tonic and the sweet Marlboro burn had rendered me into a safe place, where I wasn't alone, where a beautiful wife and a gaggle of amazing kids were tumbling around in the playroom while Daddy had some quality time alone in his screening room. (Would you like to be lonely? In a screening room, see a movie by yourself.) At times like these, when the haze was thickest, I might fantasize my life wasn't riddled with holes, that the minefield that was my past had been metal-detected and turned into a benign and lovely safety.

But back in 1999, my "person from Porlock" had sent me a script with potential that even I could see, and that potential was that none other than Bruce Willis was connected.

There was no larger cinematic star at the turn of the century than Bruce Willis. Look Who's Talking and its sequel, the Die Hard franchise, Pulp Fiction.... Nobody was more successful back then. Not to mention a pleasant change from the seventy-two romantic comedies I'd just finished. Mitchell Kapner had created a humorous script that was full of twists and turns, and it was simple to read: usually a good sign. Best of all, Bruce Willis appeared in it, and I played the starring role. I'll show you a disappointed wannabe movie star if you show me an acclaimed and prosperous TV star.

The next night, I went to Citrus on Melrose. This was the Hollywood restaurant back then: pricey, exclusive, jacket required, and a queue of paparazzi at the door clicking away wildly at everyone who arrived and went. That night, the comings and goings were myself; the film's director, Jonathan Lynn, a short round British man who'd filmed My Cousin Vinny and who happened to be Oliver Sacks's cousin; and one of the film's producers, Bruce's brother, David (David has the hair, Bruce has the chin).

Jonathan and David were relieved as they chuckled. The "dinner" was eventually over. "Well, you're our guy—we really want you to do this," Jonathan said. I rushed into my forest-green Porsche and squealed away, hands shook and cameras disregarded.

I'm going to be the lead in a Bruce Willis film, I thought as all the lights on Sunset turned green once more. Back at Carla Ridge, the moon had risen, lonely and sorrowful, casting an odd and awkward shadow across my perspective. I turned on the television, poured a vodka tonic, and waited.

The stars were aligning once more; had Matthew Perry's meteoric climb just taken another enormous leap forward? This was my thought as I watched the stars rise in a clean, dark sky. I began to count them, despite knowing the myth that once you reach a hundred, you die.

"This is Bruce Willis, Matthew." Call me back, or I'll burn down your house, shatter both your knees and arms, and leave you with just stubs for hands and feet for the rest of your life."

Bruce Willis did not disappoint—he exuded A-list glamor. He didn't simply take over a room; he became the room. In fact, I realized he was a real movie star when he showed the bartender how to prepare the ideal vodka tonic.

Bruce was forty-four years old, unmarried (he was divorced from Demi Moore at the time I met him), and he knew exactly how to make the ideal cocktail. He was at a party, and being near him was energizing. After a while, Joe Pesci, whom Jonathan Lynn had directed in My Cousin Vinny, and several very lovely women paid us a visit in our own little room. Bruce chuckled at all my stupid jokes—he appeared to love the spectacle of a younger, funnier guy showing him respect and keeping up with his drinking (if only he knew). I was delighted to be in his company since he knew how to enjoy life.

The dawn eventually came up, as it always does, and we said our blurry goodbyes. I recall thinking as I drove home, "Watch this guy—this is how to be happy." Nothing appeared to upset Bruce, and no one refused him. This was the A-leagues, after all.

So, I'd obtained The Whole Nine Yards and formed a friendship with the world's most famous movie star, but I realized I was drinking way too much to pull off this movie. Extreme measures would be required. Some people could party all night and still show up for work—but they weren't addicted like me.

The role itself was simple. All I had to do was pretend to be terrified of Bruce, which was simple, and pretend to be in love with Natasha Henstridge, which was even simpler. The director, Jonathan, whom I had nicknamed "Sammy" for some inexplicable reason, operated the type of set I enjoy—a very creative one. The funniest joke, regardless of origin, would be chosen, exactly like we did on Friends.

Every day, with me nursing a nasty hangover but still young enough to deal, we'd convene and look at the sides (TV and movie jargon for the day's work). "We" were me, Jonathan Lynn, Bruce Willis, and the funny Kevin Pollak, who played another crime leader, Janni Gogolak. It was almost like a writers' room—we'd talk about what may be humorous, what might belong here or there in a scene. A significant amount of effort was expended to include physical comedy for me to perform. I'd rush into windows and bang into doors. I once performed a take in which I spot a criminal, then turn, run into someone, get knocked back, crash into a lamp, pick up the lamp, and use it to protect myself from the baddie. Everything I came up with worked perfectly.

I only wanted to be Bruce Willis' pal after the veil was lifted. I didn't want to be like everyone else and be a suck-up to him. We had a three-day weekend while filming The Whole Nine Yards, and he flew Renee and me, as well as him and his girlfriend, to his house in Turks and Caicos. It's a lovely spot with a wonderful view of the ocean. They'd even considered purchasing all of the adjacent properties so that the paparazzi couldn't get their images. We took umbrellas with us all weekend to keep the sun off our faces and keep us from becoming too tanned for the movie. Mr. Willis taught me a new movie star trick, one of many.

But there was a significant difference between Bruce and myself. Bruce was a party animal, while I was a drug addict. Bruce has an on/off switch. He can party hard, then get a script like The Sixth Sense, quit partying, and nail the movie sober. He lacks the gene and is not an addict. There are many instances in Hollywood of people who can party and still function—I was not one of them. When I was drinking and using, if a cop came to my house and said, "If you drink tonight, you're going to jail tomorrow," I'd start packing for jail because once I start, I can't stop. All I could control was the first sip. All bets were off after that. (See also: The guy takes the booze, and the drink takes everything else.) I am no longer responsible for my behavior once I believe the lie that I can only have one drink. I need individuals, treatment centers, hospitals, and nurses to assist me.

This was excellent praise for someone who admired Tom. Bruce wasn't convinced the picture would work at all, and I'd bet him it would—if he lost, he'd have to do a guest appearance on Friends (he appears in three episodes of season six).

For three weeks, The Whole Nine Yards was the number one movie in America.

I'd done it—the dream I'd had since ninth grade had finally come true: The Whole Nine Yards wasn't Back to the Future, but Michael J. Fox and I are the only two people who have had the number one movie and TV program at the same time.

Four years after The Whole Nine Yards, Bruce, Kevin, and I shot a sequel (this time with a different director). If The Whole Nine Yards was the beginning of my movie success, The Whole Ten Yards was the end.

When The Whole Nine Yards came out, I was so engulfed in addiction that I couldn't even leave my room. My messed-up psyche has been dragging my body down with it into a hellhole of despair and demoralization. It recently occurred to me that this type of sensation should have been reserved for the release of The Whole Ten Yards. Anyone in their right mind would have been devastated by that one.

At the end of the night, when the sun was just about to rise and everyone else had left, and the celebration had come to an end, Bruce and I would just sit and talk. That's when I saw the true Bruce Willis—a kind-hearted, caring, selfless man. A fantastic parent. And a fantastic actor. Most importantly, he's a nice guy. And if he wanted me to, I would be his lifelong friend. But, as with so many of these things, our paths never met again after that.

Of course, I now pray for him every night.

Something happened that caused me to relapse. As I have stated, all it takes to relapse is something—anything—happening. Whatever the case may be.

I felt physically destroyed... but the detox was going nicely. That's what my father and the sober buddy thought. What they didn't realize was that I had a bottle of Xanax hidden in my bedroom. This is what being an addict is like: you do things you never thought you'd do. My beloved father had dropped everything to move in, to love and support me through yet another self-inflicted calamity, and I had repaid him by hiding drugs in my nightstand.

One night, I was desperate for sleep, any kind of relief from the grueling detox I was undergoing. That Xanax bottle was calling to me like an evil beacon in the night. I compared it to a lighthouse, although in this case, I turned my boat toward the crashing rocks rather than away from them. This youngster was unafraid of the childproof bottle cap; in the other room, that child's father rested, watching Taxi repeats, while in my room, beside the figurative fatal cliffs, I plunged into that bottle of Xanax and took four. (One was excessive. However, four?)

I exited my bedroom and entered the kaleidoscope of color that is my living room. Is this the afterlife? I pondered. Is this what heaven is like because the Xanax killed me last night? I calmly described what I had done to my father and the sober buddy. They were both understandably afraid. The sober buddy acted quickly and dialed 911.

At this moment, the sober friend returned to the room and expressed his regret while still offering to assist me. But I needed to visit a doctor immediately. We set out to see him. I apologized to the doctor at the end of the consultation, shook his hand, and swore it would never happen again. And I meant it when I said I was done. The doctor prescribed new detox medications as well as anti-seizure medication (Xanax withdrawal can cause seizures). We returned home. Moira, my patient assistant, was summoned to pick up the prescription, and we waited. And then I waited. This new mission took her hours to complete for some reason.

But the clock was ticking. If I didn't obtain this detox medication soon, something bad was going to happen. I might have a seizure; I might die. Neither choice appealed to me. Three grown guys were now staring at the front door, waiting for it to open, and two of them were also staring at terrified Matty.

So there you have it—the lowest point in my life. This is a classic moment for an addict, one in which they seek long-term therapy.... But wait, what's this? I noticed a crinkle in the air as I sat there looking into the kitchen. Someone who wasn't at their lowest point could have dismissed it as insignificant, but it was so intriguing to me that I couldn't turn away. It seemed like a small wave in the air. Nothing like it had ever happened to me before. It was genuine, authentic, palpable, and physical. Is this what you're looking at at the end? Was I going to die? And then...

My blood had not yet been replaced by warm honey. I was toasty, honey. And for the first time in my life, I was surrounded by love and acceptance, and I had the overpowering impression that everything would be fine. My prayer had been answered, I knew. I was in God's presence. Bill Wilson, the founder of Alcoholics Anonymous, was saved by a lightning-bolt-through-the-window experience in which he felt he was meeting God.

I began to cry. I mean, I started crying—that overwhelming, shoulder-shaking type of crying. I wasn't crying out of sadness. I was crying because I felt OK for the first time in my life. I felt safe and cared for. Decades of wrestling with God, life, and misery were being swept away, like a river of pain flowing into oblivion.

I had been in God's presence. I was sure of it. And this time I prayed for the correct thing: assistance.

Nowadays, when a particular darkness strikes me, I wonder whether it was just Xanax craziness, a continuation of the snake I was expecting to see—the medicine can trigger what the National Institutes of Health call "reversible brief psychotic episodes." (I later had a massive seizure in front of my father, which wasn't the greatest pleasure I've ever had—neither was being rushed to UCLA Medical Center, which I thought was an angel way station at the time.) But I swiftly return to the golden light's truth. Even when I'm sober, I can see it and remember what it did for me. Some may dismiss it as a near-death experience, but I was present, and it was God. And when I am connected, God shows me that it was genuine in small ways, as when the sunshine touches the water and turns it a beautiful golden color. Or when I watch the light return to someone's eyes as they emerge from the darkness into sobriety, or when I see the reflection of sunlight on the green leaves of a tree. And I feel it when I help someone get sober, the way their gratitude warms my heart. Because they are unaware that I should be thanking them.

A year later, I met the woman I'd be with for the next six years. God is all around you; you simply have to clear your channel or you'll miss it.

Chapter 7
The Benefit of Friends

Monica was the first to go, and she placed her key on the vacant counter. Chandler was the next to leave. Then came Joey, who should not have had a key in the first place, followed by Ross, Rachel, and finally Phoebe. What do you say now that there are six keys on the countertop?

The truth was that we were all eager for Friends to end. For starters, Jennifer Aniston had decided she no longer wanted to do the show, and because we all made decisions as a group, we all had to stop. Jennifer wanted to do movies; I had been doing movies all that time and had The Whole Ten Yards, which was sure to be a hit (insert donkey's head now), but even though it had been the best job in the world, the stories of Monica, Chandler, Joey, Ross, Rachel, and Phoebe had all pretty much played out by 2004. It was not lost on me that Chandler had matured far faster than I had. As a result, ten was a brief season, mostly by Jenny's design. But by this point, all of the characters were fundamentally happy, and no one wants to see a bunch of happy people doing happy things—what's funny about that?

The date was January 23, 2004. The keys on the counter, a man who resembled Chandler Bing replied, "Where?," The song "Embryonic Journey" by Jefferson Airplane played as the camera panned to the rear of the apartment door, and Ben, our first AD and very close friend, exclaimed for the final time, "That's a wrap," and tears sprang from practically everyone's eyes like geysers. We'd made 237 episodes, including this one, suitably titled "The Last One." Aniston was sobbing, and I was surprised she had any water left in her body after a long time. Even Matt LeBlanc was in tears. But I didn't feel anything; I wasn't sure if it was due to the opioid buprenorphine I was taking, or if I was just dead inside. (For the record, buprenorphine is an amazing detox medication that is intended to help you stay off other "stronger" opiates—it does not modify you in any way. However, it is the most difficult drug in the world to quit. Bupe, also known as Suboxone, should never be used for more than seven days at a time. I had been on it for eight months because I was afraid of a bad detox.)

I remembered having to ask the producers to let me stop speaking like Chandler for the last several seasons (not to mention getting rid of those sweater vests). That specific cadence—could it be more annoying?—had become so ingrained that I thought I'd explode if I had to put the emphasis in the wrong place one more time, so I just went back to saying lines normally, for the most part in season six and beyond.

I remembered crying when I asked Monica to marry me.

Friends had been a safe haven, a source of solace for me; they had given me a reason to get out of bed every morning, as well as a reason to take it a little easy the night before. We were having the time of our lives. It seemed like we got some wonderful news every day. Even I realized that only a madman (which I have been at times) could mess up a job like that.

My future, even without Friends, seems bright enough. I had a major film coming out; I'd done two episodes of Ally McBeal and three episodes of The West Wing, so I was gaining serious acting chops as well as humor (I'd received two Emmy nods for my three The West Wing appearances). I'd also recently wrapped The Ron Clark Story, a TNT film about a real-life small-town teacher who gets a job in one of Harlem's worst schools. There wasn't a single joke in the entire movie, which drove me insane, so off camera I developed a character named "Ron Dark" who was drunk and continually swore in front of the children. Despite this, it was a huge success when it finally broadcast in August 2006. I'd be nominated for a SAG award, a Golden Globe award, and an Emmy. (I was defeated by Robert Duvall in all three. I couldn't believe I'd been beaten out by such a jerk.)

But, as I previously stated, The Whole Ten Yards would be a flop—I doubt even my closest family and friends saw it. In fact, if you looked closely enough at the premiere, you could see people avoiding their gaze from the screen. I believe it has a 0 rating on Rotten Tomatoes.

That was the moment Hollywood decided not to cast Mr. Perry in any more films.

I had planned to attend a 12-step meeting the day following the final episode of Friends, with the intention of starting my new life on the right foot. But facing a blank canvas of an empty day was extremely difficult for me. I awoke the next morning wondering, "What the fuck am I going to do now?"

Then I was single once more.

With no tremendously high-paying, dream-come-true job to go to and no special someone in my life, things deteriorated quickly—it seemed like I was going down a cliff. The lunacy of utilizing additional, heavier substances seeped back into my twisted mind. It wasn't long before the seemingly unthinkable occurred once more. I began drinking and using.

I was also hurting from loneliness; I could feel it in my bones. On the outside, I appeared to be the luckiest guy alive, so I could only complain to a few people without being ordered to shut up, and even then... nothing could fill the emptiness inside me. I once purchased yet another new car, the thrill of which lasted approximately five days. I moved frequently as well—the excitement of a new house with an even better view lasted slightly longer than the Porsche or Bentley, but not by much. I was also so introspective that having a true give-and-take relationship with a woman was nearly impossible; I was much better at friends with benefits, so whoever I was seeing didn't discover that insidious, creeping feeling that I was irredeemably not enough.

I was a man in desperate need of a yellow light experience, so I will be eternally grateful that it happened in my house that day, because it gave me a new lease on life. I'd been given the gift of sobriety yet again. The only question was, what would I do with it? Nothing has ever worked in the long run. I'd have to change my approach to everything or I'd be toast. And I didn't want to be one of them. Not until I had learned to live and love. Not until the world began to make more sense to me.

My habit would have killed the wrong person if it had killed me. I wasn't totally myself yet; I was only parts of myself (and not always the nicest parts). My new way of life would have to begin with work, because it appeared to be the simplest place to begin. Accepting effort was my only hope. I got some sober time in and was able to get back on my feet. I also had a few friends-with-benefits relationships going on, one of which was gradually evolving into something more. Perhaps much more. I'd made friends with benefits before, but this? This was less evident to me. "Why don't you stick around and we can watch a movie?" I began to want her to stay past the sex.

What was I up to? I was breaking every rule.

When we first met, she was twenty-three and I was thirty-six. In reality, I knew she was 23 since I had crashed her 23rd birthday party. Our first make-out session was in the backseat of a filthy Toyota (to think I'd spent all that money on nice automobiles and now I'm in the backseat of a tan Corolla). "I'm getting out of the car now," I said when we were finished. "It's mostly because I'm 36."

So began two years of potentially record-breaking sexual intercourse with no strings attached, both of us strictly adhering to the guidelines of friends-with-benefits. We were on the same wavelength. We never went out to eat or chatted about each other's families. We never talked about what was going on in each other's life with relation to other people. It was texting instead, with stuff like, "How about Thursday night at seven?"

It didn't seem like a wild move because I had dabbled in it with fantastic results on The West Wing, Ally McBeal, and The Ron Clark Story. I tried out for a few serious films but didn't get any of them. I shot a couple indie films that tried hard but didn't work out.

I'd never seen so much passion directed at a project—it was magnetic. The sequel to their hit show The West Wing, Studio 60 on the Sunset Strip, was written by Aaron Sorkin and directed by Thomas Schlamme. They had almost fifteen Emmys between them, so their new endeavor created a frenzy in the fall of 2005 unlike anything before. I'd never seen a project with that much power behind it before it even began. To get that thing, NBC and CBS fought like gladiators, with NBC eventually winning out for something like $3 million per episode. Everywhere I looked that fall, someone was talking about Studio 7 on the Sunset Strip (its original name). I was wrapping up writing The Ron Clark Story in New York and staying at my favorite hotel in the world, the Greenwich in Tribeca. I was eager to read this fantastic script. I waited because the script would not arrive at my hotel until 10:00 p.m. because I was on the East Coast.

Studio 60 on the Sunset Strip had a fatal weakness that no amount of superb writing, direction, or performance could overcome. The stakes were as high as you could imagine on The West Wing: a nuclear weapon is aiming toward Ohio, and the president has to solve that shit? People in Ohio would watch such a show merely to see what would happen if they were encouraged to kiss their own asses goodbye by an impending intercontinental ballistic missile.

A very limited group of people, including myself, understand that getting a joke right is a matter of life and death in a certain industry. These are warped, strange folks. People in Canton, Ohio, watching Studio 60 on the Sunset Strip, on the other hand, presumably thought, It's just a joke, why isn't everyone calm down? What's the big deal, what's the problem with all of you? This was not the Monty Python sketch about Ernest Scribbler writing a joke so amusing that it murdered Nazis. (Because they don't know German, the British are immune to its force. And the killer joke's actual German is nonsense, which is equally amusing.) There may have been a loyal audience in Rock Center or at the Comedy Store on Sunset, but the main premise of the act didn't reach the levels of edge-of-your-seat stakes. Trying to tie the stakes of The West Wing to a comedic program would never succeed.

I also had a different perspective on the creative process in general—I was used to offering ideas, but Aaron rejected all of them. I had opinions about my character's arc as well, but they were not welcomed. The issue is that I'm not just a talking head. I have a brain, especially when it comes to comedy. Aaron Sorkin is a far better writer than I am, but he is not a funnier man (he once claimed that Friends was his favorite show). In Studio 60, I played a comedy writer. I thought I had some amusing ideas, but Aaron said no to all of them. That's his prerogative, and it's no reflection on him that he prefers to do his set in this manner. It simply disappointed me. (Aaron did the same thing to Tom Hanks, according to him.)

I'd paid a lot of money for an artist to paint the two of us for Christmas. Our relationship had always been sex- and text-driven—at least for the first four years—and I'd learned from my company manager that we'd exchanged around 1,780 texts. So, in the painting, there she was, sitting down with a copy of The New York Times and some bottled water, as she always did, and there I was, wearing a long sleeve T-shirt with another T-shirt on top, as I always did, holding a Red Bull and reading a Sports Illustrated... We were texting each other the entire time. The artist had added 1,780 hearts, one for each phrase, then smashed them all together to form a single large heart. I'd never spent so much money on a present before. I adored her and wanted her to know it.

My objective was to present her with the painting before asking her the question. You know the one; I'm not going to tell you how it goes, especially because... well, I never asked. When I gave her the gift, she was moved, saying, "Matty, my little heart—what you're doing to my little heart."

And the time had come. "Honey, I love you," was all I had to say. Will you..." But I didn't say anything. All my concerns reared up like a serpent, the snake I dreaded would come after me the year before I met her, the period when I'd seen God but didn't learn enough from him.

I got into Chandler fucking Bing mode right away.

I had missed the opportunity. Who knows, maybe she was anticipating it. I'd been seconds; seconds and a lifetime away. If I'd asked, now we'd have two kids and a house with no view, who knows—I wouldn't need the view since I'd have her to look at, as well as the kids. Instead, I'm some schmuck sitting alone in his house at fifty-three, staring down at a hushed sea....

So I didn't inquire. I was either too terrified, too shattered, or too bent. I'd been completely faithful to her for the entire time, including the last two years, during which I didn't want to have sex with her for some reason, during which no amount of couples therapy could explain why I'd never asked the damn question, and why I now only saw her as my best friend. My pal; my dearest pal. And I didn't want to lose my best friend, so I tried for two years to make it work.

I had no idea why the sex had ceased. I have this creeping, nagging, never-ending concern that if we grew any closer, she'd see the true me and leave me. I didn't like myself at the time, you see. Our age gap had also become an issue. She was always wanting to get out and do things, but I desired a more established life.

Mr. Sunshine is a TV show I produced. I believe that life is about the journey, not the destination, and because I had not yet written, this was my first attempt. Writing a network show about something you want to write about is nearly impossible. There are so many cooks in the kitchen—executives and other writers who all want a say—that the reality of your true vision getting to the screen is reserved only for someone like Sorkin.

Mr. Sunshine revolves around my character, Ben Donovan, who owns and operates a sports facility in San Diego; Allison Janney plays my supervisor. One of Ben's major flaws is his unwillingness to make himself attractive to women.... After the titles, I even managed to get in an inside joke: my production firm was called "Anhedonia Productions," and the ad card we designed included a cartoon of me moaning with boredom on a roller coaster. Despite my efforts, the show was a tremendous hit for about two weeks before everyone in the world decided they didn't want to watch it.

I'd Go On to make another program (oh, yeah, that's what it was called, Go On) about a sports talk radio broadcaster dealing with the loss of his wife. NBC kept promoting it, even airing it during the Olympics, and sixteen million people saw the premiere. But a comedy about bereavement counseling? The finale drew only 2.5 million viewers in April 2013. Once again, a production I was directing had a fantastic opening but was canceled. I relapsed once more because I had nothing to do and no one to love. But I noticed this one soon and checked into a recovery facility in Utah.

I was sitting in my room in the New York rehab facility, craving opiates. My body was screaming for narcotics since the detox hadn't worked. I told the doctor and the counselor, but I really didn't need to—I was trembling and shivering, visibly withdrawing.

If you left the premises, you had to undergo a pee test right away when you returned. So I went outside, met the vehicle, passed up some money, got some tablets, and they drove away. Back at the treatment center, I went straight to the bathroom, passed the urine test, and ingested three medications.

The following morning, at 10:00 a.m., all the powers that be in this horrible place had convened in a circle. Their message was straightforward: you're fired.

However, I was hooked on six milligrams of Ativan at the time, and this new place did not provide Ativan, which the New York location could have checked on but did not. My own experiences, as well as years of interactions with other addicts, have led me to feel that the majority of these places are shitholes in any case. They are hell-bent on exploiting sick and vulnerable individuals and cashing paychecks. The entire system is corrupt and messed up.

Chapter 8
Trauma Camp

After Friends, after the movies, after that six-year relationship, after the collapse and rise and rise and fall—after everything—I found myself on an odyssey for the next six years. Contrary to popular belief, I was not a wealthy guy with nothing to do; in fact, I had more to do than before. No, I was a man tumbling down a slope, stranded in a roaring river, attempting to find refuge on any safe and dry rock.

I'd gone to Cirque Lodge in Sun Valley, Utah, between Mr. Sunshine and Go On—rehab number three, if you're keeping score at home. The Lodge is located in the Utah Rockies, near the base of Mount Timpanogos. I'm not a great fan of nature—in terms of peace and quiet, I prefer the beach, or at least a glimpse of the water—but this spot was breathtaking. The air was pure and thin, razor-sharp and clarifying. There were turkeys everywhere, gobbling to the bone (and flying once in a while—who knew they could fly?), golden eagles, and on some days, a moose would pass by, heavy and slow (no, I wasn't hallucinating; there were moose there).

It was customary for participants to invite friends to come and visit during Family and Friends Week, but I resisted. My father had visited me at Hazelden, my mother at Promises Malibu, and my then-girlfriend had spent many hours watching me rant with a slew of house nurses and sober companions while detoxing. I didn't want to subject them to this again. It was too terrible, too difficult, and too unfair. It was the least I could do to give them a rest. I'd put myself into this mess, and I'd get myself out of it.

But one day, around Friends and Family Week, I found myself sitting outside by myself, hoping to see a moose or a bird flapping up into the trees. The day was bitterly cold, subzero, but I needed to smoke, so there was nothing for it except to bundle up and deal.... A light snow began to fall while I sat there puffing on a Marlboro, creating an intense quiet, as if the cosmos was patiently listening to my thoughts and emotions.

In fact, I was living in a society where, despite its neutrality, I had managed to carve out an important, meaningful place for myself. I needed to know that when I died, I didn't want my Friends to be toward the bottom of my list of accomplishments. I needed to remind myself to be courteous to people, to make their bumping into me a pleasant experience rather than one that filled me with dread, as if that was all that counted. I needed to be more kind, to love more deeply, to listen more carefully, and to give unreservedly. It was time to quit being such a fearful asshole and accept that I would be able to manage whatever problems arose. Because I was powerful.

The snow eventually stopped falling, and a moose crept gently into the gardens. That lengthy face seemed placid, as if it had seen everything at least once and wasn't fazed by anything. That had a lesson in it, I reasoned. A few calves kept up with her, full of the vitality that only children have. They all gazed at me as they sat in the twilight, then turned and walked away.

I left Cirque Lodge lean and joyful, eager to take on the world and spend the rest of my life with my love. But my then-girlfriend didn't like this new Matty—I got the impression she didn't enjoy the fact that I needed her less than before. Perhaps my issues had given her a false sense of security. This guy will never leave me, not while he is so preoccupied with his own issues. She didn't like the fact that I was better. That unpleasant truth proved to be our undoing. We gave up after trying so hard to fit the individual pieces together. Everything was depressing. She was my absolute favorite person in the world, but it was not to be. It was the proper thing to do, but it wasn't without sadness.

I'd spent time at Promises, a rehab in Malibu, in 2001 (just after picking up AA's Big Book in Marina del Rey). I met a guy named Earl H. there. He'd been teaching a class at Promises, and I'd loved him right away. He was amusing and quite informed about AA. He also had a few other celebrity clients who were doing well, so I figured he'd be my guy and asked him to sponsor me. (He claimed he hadn't drank since 1980.) Over coffee, I confessed that one of my fears was that he'd pass me a script to read one day. He went on to say, "Well, there is a script, but I wouldn't do that to you...."

So our connection began. I practiced the steps with him, even chasing him down to complete them. I was so desperate to get into the program and stay sober that I called him every day and asked for a job. Nobody had ever followed him harder, he claimed, and over the next ten years, he came to wear two hats—he was my sponsor, but he was also my best friend. I turned to face him and listened to him. We had the same sense of humor and even sounded similar. I ignored the idea that he was somewhat famous in the rehab world, a world where everything should be kept private.

But my biggest blunder was that I had made him my higher authority. If I had a problem with a relationship or anything else, I would call him, and he would be extremely wise about it. It got to the point where if he'd said, "I'm sorry, Matthew, but you have to move to Alaska and stand on your head," I'd have booked a ticket to Anchorage right now. If he'd said, "You can eat nothing but green M&M's for the next three months," you could bet I'd be shitting khaki.

Then our friendship evolved into a business. Yes, I started a business with my sponsor. Fucking fatal error.

Earl had founded a corporation that would build and operate sober living homes throughout Los Angeles. I put $500,000 into the firm and converted my Malibu home into Perry House, a sober living facility. Earl and I traveled to Washington, DC multiple times to speak with lawmakers to promote the efficacy of drug courts, at the request of a terrific person named West Huddleston, the head of the National Association of Drug Court Professionals. Drug courts seek to decriminalize nonviolent addicts by providing them with care and therapy rather than jail time. Gil Kerlikowske, then Obama's "drug czar," even managed to award me a "Champion of Recovery award" from the Obama administration's Office of National Drug Control Policy in May 2013. At the time, I quipped to The Hollywood Reporter that "had I been arrested, I would be sitting in prison somewhere with a tattoo on my face."

Earl had been scheduled to come on Piers Morgan with me but had backed out at the last minute. Nonetheless, we later traveled to Europe to increase the power of drug courts, and I had the opportunity to debate the matter on a late-night BBC news show called Newsnight. There was the moderator, Jeremy Paxman, who was known for being unpleasant to guests; Baroness Meacher, who was the then-chair of the UK All-Party Parliamentary Group on Drug Policy Reform and was very much on my side; and then a complete tool named Peter Hitchens.

I asked Earl for my money back at lunch, and I'm still waiting. He was fantasizing of being an actress, among other things. Something was wrong, and I was so spooked out by it all that I went home and used it. This was entirely my fault, but two things were irreversibly lost: my innocence and my faith in Earl H.

Earl eventually moved to Arizona without telling me, and our friendship ended. I'd lost half a million dollars, my closest ally, and the innocence I'd cherished all those years by sharing our lives and being best friends and pushing for drug courts and constructing a sober living home. Heartbreak.

I was furious with myself for what had transpired on CBS's The Odd Couple. I'd been a tremendous fan of the film adaptation of Neil Simon's play for a long time and had always wanted to develop a new TV version of it. My goal came true in 2013, when CBS approved the concept. Go On, my previous show before The Odd Couple, had failed, but I was more certain about this one. The original material was amazing, the cast was fantastic, and everything was in place for a hit. Nonetheless, despair followed me, and my addictions returned in full force. As a result, I'm deeply humiliated by my actions on The Odd Couple. On top of the severe sadness, I was always late and high, and I eventually lost control of the program to a showrunner. But I accept full responsibility for what transpired and would like to apologize to everyone involved, not just my fellow castmates.

I'd been inspired by—and by inspired, I mean I was aiming to beat—Sexual Perversity in Chicago, and I was pleased with my results. I'd take it over that wonderful play any day. "There's a very popular notion that people don't change," I'd told The Hollywood Reporter, "but I see people change every day, and I wanted to put that message out there while making people laugh." As a result, the play opens with four buddies in a bar seeking to find love—my character, Jack, begins the play as an egomaniac who also happens to be an alcoholic, and things only go worse from there.

We debuted in the Playhouse Theatre, a facility with a capacity of 800 people, and promptly sold out. In fact, we were breaking box office records while also receiving poor reviews. There were seven important reviews for historical accuracy, six of which were negative. The thought of a Hollywood actor-boy performing a play in London did not sit well with London critics. But it was a big hit, and I was a playwright who liked the notion.

There was also one person who refused to attend the play, despite my entreaties.

The woman I'd dated for six years was now dating a British guy, and they were splitting their time between London and Los Angeles. We'd had a few meals and texted a few times while we were still friendly. I'd offered to see The End of Longing when she was in London, but she'd texted back saying she was far too busy. "I'll see you Stateside!" she wrote. I answered that I was disappointed that she couldn't make it—the play was being played in her town, for God's sake—and then I received an email saying that she was getting married and that she had no room in her life for friends.

After you've gone back into the trauma and relieved it, the therapists are supposed to "close" you up again—basically, you're supposed to feel everything, release it, and learn how to make it a story, not a living thing in your soul, so it no longer has dominion over you in the way that it did.

They didn't properly close me up, and I didn't cry. I was terrified. I felt as if I were back onstage. Being famous in rehab may not be what you expect—everyone else there has a lot on their plate, so who cares if you're Matthew Perry? Later, in Pennsylvania, I went to a rehabilitation center with six other individuals in their seventies, including Debbie, aka the bane of my existence. Debbie was the only other smoker, so I had to keep an eye on her all the time. Debbie, on the other hand, had no memories.

Chapter 9
Violence in Hollywood

When a guy or woman asks me to assist them in quitting drinking, and I do so, seeing as the light gradually returns to their eyes, that's all God to me. And, despite having a relationship with God and being grateful despite everything, I sometimes want to tell God to go fuck himself for making my path so difficult.

I'm no saint—none of us are—but if you've been on the verge of death and don't die, you'd think you'd be filled with relief and thanks. But that isn't the case; instead, you are irritated by the difficult path ahead of you to become healthier. Something else occurs as well. You're troubled with the question, "Why have I been spared?" The other four patients on the ECMO machine had died as well. There had to be a purpose for this.

My romantic life, on the other hand, is a different tale. In my romantic life, I've made more blunders than Elizabeth Taylor. I am a romantic and passionate individual. I've yearned for love; it's a want in me that I can't quite put my finger on.

The regulations had changed by the time I was in my forties. I'd done all the sleeping with individuals I'd ever need to do—now I needed a partner, a comrade, someone to share my life with. In addition, I have always adored children. I believe it's because my sister Caitlin was born when I was eleven years old. Then came Emily, Will, and, eventually, Madeline. I like playing with them all, babysitting them and making up silly games with them. A child's laughter is the most beautiful sound in the world.

So, by the time I was in my forties, I really wanted a girlfriend, someone I could rely on and who, in turn, could rely on me. One night, some friends and I went out to celebrate yet another year of sobriety. David Pressman, a long-time friend of mine, introduced me to his girlfriend's sister, Laura. We'd all gone to a Dodgers game together, but there was no game, no stadium, no hot dog vendors for me—the world had receded to a lovely face hidden beneath a baseball cap. I attempted to use my old Perry charm—anything to get her attention—but she was too preoccupied with flaunting her amazing personality and wit to others. She was underwhelmed that I was Chandler, and though she was absolutely cordial to me, I had the impression she didn't have a there-there.

The gang had opted to play Ping-Pong at the Standard Hotel in downtown Los Angeles this time. Now, I'm no Forrest Gump, but I can play Ping-Pong—in fact, if you've seen the season nine finale of Friends, you'll know I'm good enough to beat Paul Rudd. I knew Laura may show up, so I played Ping-Pong while keeping one eye on the door.

Finally, she appeared. She was all energy and humor, as if she had been thrown into the club by a whirlwind.

Our first date took place on New Year's Eve. I asked Laura to a pajama party that a buddy was throwing. After that, our relationship grew slowly; she was cautious, and I was eager to go to any length. But our feelings grew stronger. It was all good... but nothing is ever perfect in my world, remember?

Enter the city of Rome. I had been clean for two years and was prospering in AA, healthy, sponsoring people, and developing a TV show. I was ecstatic, even muscular, dare I say. (I dare: I'd been working out in the gym!) I was requested to speak at an AA meeting in West Hollywood, and you can't say no to an AA request. The place was full, with standing room only (I believe news had spread that I was speaking). My story had not yet reached the depths of the last few years, so in addition to recounting everything I'd gone through, I was able to get my fair share of chuckles. I went over to the kitchen area at one point and spotted a woman peering through the window/hatch contraption, leaning on her elbows to prop herself up. She was stunningly attractive and like a wonderful porcelain doll. There were suddenly only two people in the room. My AA contribution became solely aimed at Rome. It turned out to be one of the best shares I'd ever given since this magnificent beauty captivated me so much that I wanted her to know everything about me. I wanted her to be aware of everything.

What about Laura, though? Yes, of course, gorgeous Laura, whom I am growing more fond of by the day. But now we have Rome. What is a guy to do? Forget about Rome and keep looking into this Laura thing that is going so beautifully. Right? That's what a reasonable person would do in these circumstances.

I told myself that I wasn't being an asshole because I hadn't told either Laura or Rome that we were in a relationship, but there was a part of me that knew I was doing something wrong because I cared about both of them, and despite outward appearances, I genuinely didn't want anyone to get hurt, including myself. So Laura and I would go to Kings games together, laugh, and have a fantastic, albeit somewhat chaste, time. The relationship with both ladies was sluggish at first, but they ultimately lifted their sex embargoes, and I was now totally involved with two distinct women at the same time. It was incredible, as well as perplexing and bizarre.

What did I intend to do? I had a great time with both of them. They were fantastic. This carried on for almost six months before I realized I needed to choose one. I had to put an end to this madness and choose one. Rome was passionate, sexy, humorous, and intelligent, but she also seemed to have a preoccupation with death, which perplexed me. Laura talked about movies and lighter topics; she made me feel at ease in a way that Rome had not.

I made the tough phone call to Rome. She was OK about it at first, until she wasn't, yelling at me for two hours in the parking lot of Barney's Beanery on Santa Monica Boulevard when I tried to make amends. You'd be hard pressed to find an angrier person than she was that day with me.

There was an alternative. I could stay in the relationship while returning to drugs and attempting to maintain a low habit. This would shield me from the fear, allowing me to let down my guard and get more personal with her.

For me, turning to narcotics has resulted in nothing but mayhem. And yet, inexplicably, I chose to do it again to deal with the Laura problem. I began taking one tablet every day just to stay in the relationship. It was amazing at first, but as is always the case with drugs, they inevitably win. We had a shitstorm on our hands six months later. I was in shambles. Laura broke up with me, so I had to restart Suboxone and enter into a sober living facility. I was terrified that I was going to die again. Rome was still ranting at me whenever she could, and Laura was wounded, worried, and gone.

You lose both of them.

So there I was, living in a sober living house in Malibu on 8 milligrams of Suboxone. Though it is a great detox drug—the best, in my opinion—it is the most difficult drug to go off of. In fact, coming off it made me suicidal. That's not entirely accurate—I had suicidal thoughts, but I also realized it was just the medicine, so I wasn't genuinely suicidal. All I had to do was wait out the days when I felt suicidal, do nothing about it, and trust that eventually I would feel better and no longer want to kill myself.

Seven years later, after learning a lot about myself, I made genuine reparations to both Rome and Laura, and they both accepted my apology. Believe it or not, the three of us have become friends. Laura is married to a wonderful man named Jordan, and Rome is married to an equally wonderful man named Eric.

I am not a violent man, but I have been both a victim and perpetrator of violence once in my life.

Years ago, shortly after she ended her relationship with Justin Timberlake, I was put up on a date with Cameron Diaz.

Cameron was at a dinner party with a bunch of other people, but when she saw me, she got stoned fairly immediately—it was evident that she wasn't interested in me at all. But the party went on, and at one point we were all playing a game—I believe it was Pictionary. I remarked something humorous to Cameron as she was painting, to which she replied, "Oh, come on!" and punched me in the shoulder.

In 2004, I flew to Chris Evert's tennis academy in Florida for the Chris Evert / Bank of America Pro-Celebrity Tennis Classic, a charity tournament. It was a true Hollywood who's who. But Chevy Chase piqued my interest the most.

Chevy had long been one of my heroes. In reality, his performance in the film Fletch had irrevocably transformed my life. My best friend Matt Ondre and I went to watch a preview screening of Fletch one freezing night in LA, and we were literally rolling in the aisles with laughter at one point. Chevy must have had three hundred jokes in that film, and he hit them all wonderfully. Later, as Matt and I waited at the bus stop waiting for our trip home, I turned to him and said solemnly, "Matt, I am going to talk that way for the rest of my life." And I did. This makes the following anecdote especially unpleasant for both Chevy and myself.

My talents were admittedly rusty by this point. I hadn't played in years, and my ground strokes were in desperate need of improvement. What I did have was a really hard serve—in fact, the event had a speed clock, and I clocked it at 111 miles per hour. The only difficulty was that I had no idea where they were headed. Which was OK in a regular public court, but not so much in front of two thousand people. Former President George H. W. Bush was also present....

More specifically, his testicles did not move—I simply served something close to a professional-speed serve directly into his Chevy Chases. If you understand what I mean.

What happened next was as follows: Chevy made a goofy look, similar to the one he makes in Fletch when a doctor examines his prostate, and then fell to the ground. (Remember, this was all happening in front of two thousand people.)

After the event, four medics rushed onto the court, strapped him to a gurney, and rushed him to the nearest hospital.

Michael Keaton and Steve Martin should take cover if this is what I do to my heroes.

Chapter 10
The Big Terrible Thing

Consider this: you have to walk back onto a stage where you have literally spit the bed for weeks. You've been slurring lines and making terrible decisions. You're in New York City, and despite having not one but two sober companions, you contact room service at the hotel, your voice shaking, detoxing, and say, "Please put a bottle of vodka in my room's bathtub." The bathtub, to be precise. Put that in there."

And then, when the day is done, you go back to that fucking hotel room, drink the bottle of vodka, and you feel okay for about three hours before having to do it all over again the next day. You're trembling and pretending that you're not in serious trouble anytime you speak to anyone. You contact the hotel and instruct them to perform the vodka-bottle-in-the-bathtub thing again, using the same nervous voice.

So here I am in Dallas, on methadone, a quart of vodka every day, cocaine, and Xanax. Every day, I'd arrive on set, pass out in my chair, wake up to do a scene, stumble to set, and then scream into a camera for two minutes. Then it was back to my recliner for more snoozing.

I was one of the most renowned individuals in the world at the time, and I was being scorched by the white-hot flame of fame. As a result, no one dared to speak up about this heinous behavior. The film's producers planned to finish the picture, slap my name on a banner, and make $60 million. Friends were even worse—no one wanted to interfere with that money-making machine.

But, after Jamie Tarses informed me that I was leaving, I went to rehab and eventually returned to finish the film.

This was me as I was serving Sara. I was in shambles. I felt terrible, and I apologized to everyone, and I like to think I did a fantastic job for the final thirteen days of filming. Everyone tried to be nice about it, and they did their best, but they were irritated; the director was irritated—I'd damaged his movie; Elizabeth Hurley, my co-star, was irritated (she never got to do another movie, either).

Of course, the film bombed anyway. I was paid $3.5 million to make the film, and I was sued for the shutdown, despite the fact that it was due to a medical emergency. When a team of insurance execs confronted me at the mediation table, I just wrote them a check for $650,000.

As I finished reading my list, we noticed a wedding beginning in the gardens. I watched as the newlyweds beamed at each other, the family dressed to the nines, and the officiant smiled as he prepared to ramble on about illness and health until death do them part. I hadn't been there for anyone in a long time, my addiction being my best friend, my bad friend, my punisher, and my lover all rolled into one. My major calamity. But that day, up there with the view—of course, there has to be a view—and with the soon-to-be newlyweds and Gandhi around, I felt an awakening, that I was here for more than just this great dreadful thing. That I could help and love people because, no matter how far down the scale I had fallen, I had a narrative to tell, a story that could truly help people. And assisting others has become my solution.

The top page of The New York Times on July 19, 2019 carried items about Donald Trump, Stormy Daniels, a tragic arson at a Kyoto animation studio, and Puerto Ricans who had "had enough."

I despised myself. I was on the verge of committing suicide. The embarrassment, loneliness, and sorrow were too much to bear. I just laid there, trying to deal with everything, but there was nothing I could do. It had already been completed. I was frightened of dying, which contradicted my activities.

But that was the end of it. The Matthew Perry Show has been canceled due to opiates.

I had been on and off opiates for so long that I had developed a condition that only a small percentage of the population experiences.

Constipation is caused by opiates. It's almost poetry. I was so full of crap that I almost died.

I often reflect on that time and am grateful that it occurred before Covid, because else I would have been trapped in that room for five months. As it turned out, I was never alone in that room. That was God's love manifested in human form.

My mother and I are both crisis experts at this point. What I've always wanted to tell her is that the show Friends, as well as all the other series and movies? I basically did anything for her attention. And yet, that is the one individual who did not receive much attention from Friends. She mentioned it on occasion, but she was never overjoyed with her son's accomplishments.

But I don't think she could possibly have been proud enough for what I required. And, if you're going to blame your parents for the terrible, you should equally give them credit for the good. Everything is good. I couldn't have played Chandler if my mother hadn't been my mother. I would never have made $80 million if it hadn't been for my mother. Because Chandler was only a mask for genuine pain. What a better sitcom character! Chandler began by making jokes about everything so we wouldn't have to talk about anything serious. Chandler was supposed to be "an observer of other people's lives" in the show's first description. So he'd be the man who, at the end of a play, would crack a joke or comment on whatever had just happened—the Fool in King Lear, uttering truth where none had previously existed. But everyone grew to like Chandler so much that he became his own significant character. That he ended up superseding what I did in real life—getting married, having kids— well, certain things I can't really talk about.

The simple truth is that when I was fifteen, I abandoned my mother, just as she had been abandoned by my father. I was a difficult child to deal with, and she, too, was a child. She constantly gave her all and stayed in my hospital room with me for five months following the coma.

An addict feels elated after taking medication. However, after a short time, the pill no longer makes people feel euphoric because a tolerance has developed. But the addict still desperately wants to feel euphoric, so they take two instead of one to achieve the same effect.

The UCLA hospital gave me opioids for my fabricated stomach discomfort, but I needed more, so I contacted a drug dealer. But I was on the forty-first level of that Century City building, which meant I had to find out a method to descend forty floors, give the dealer the money in an empty cigarette packet, and obtain my pills. Then I had to sneak back to the forty-first floor, take the medications, and feel better for a time.

I didn't have a choice because I was addicted to whatever they provided me. If I had just responded, "No, fuck off," it would have been a great moment, but the drugs would have stopped and I would have become quite ill. I was put in the unusual position of having to choose between being locked up in New York or Houston for months. Perhaps the decision should be made by someone more capable than me? I chose New York because I was the least qualified to make a selection.

After three nights, I met a very attractive and incredibly intelligent nurse. She took excellent care of me, and I flirted with her as much as you can with someone who changes your colostomy bag on a regular basis. The terrible day of having to quit smoking loomed, so I was allowed to go out for coffee with the great nurse. As a result, my mood improved slightly. We returned after I made jokes and flirted in the "we're all in rehab, so nothing can really happen" sort.

I stepped up to the ward and met therapists—Bruce, Wendy, whatever—who I despised. Everything I wanted to do was smoke. Or bring up the subject of smoking. Or smoke while discussing smoking.

Every day, I'm this close to death.

I don't have any more sobriety left in me. I'd never be able to return if I went out. And if I went out, I was going to go out hard. Because my tolerance is so great, I would have to go out hard.

It's not like the Amy Winehouse narrative, in which she was sober for a long time before the first drinks killed her. She expressed something in that documentary that I agree with. She had recently won a Grammy and told a buddy, "I can't enjoy this unless I'm drunk."

I had no idea what was going on when I reached fifty-five tablets each day, like the character Betsy Mallum in Dopesick. I had no idea I was addicted. I was one of the first famous people to go to rehab, and everyone knew about it. In 1997, I was on America's number one TV show and went to rehab, and it appeared on the covers of magazines. But I had no idea what was going on. In Dopesick, Betsy Mallum advances to heroin and dies—you see her nod out, grin, and die. But it's that smile that I crave all the time. She must have felt great, but it took her life. But that beatific moment is still something I crave, albeit without the death element. I'm looking for a connection. I desire that connection to something bigger than myself because I believe it is the only way to actually rescue my life.

I don't want to perish. I'm terrified of dying.

I'm not even excellent at locating the medications. Someone I worked with once introduced me to a corrupt doctor. I'd claim I had migraine headaches—actually, I had about eight doctors working on my fabricated migraines—and still had to sit through a 45-minute MRI to receive medicines. When things got very bad, I'd go to drug dealer houses. When the doctor died, his nurse took his place. She had all the medications, and she lived in the Valley, so I would go see her whenever I needed pills. I'd be scared the whole time.

When I lived in Century City, I'd make excuses to go down forty stories to score. I was extremely sick and hurt at the time—my stomach hadn't closed yet, and I was alone throughout Covid... I had a nurse on staff who gave me medicines, but I wasn't getting high anymore. So I'd phone a drug dealer and acquire some more Oxy.

This way, in addition to the meds I'd been prescribed, I'd be able to actually feel them. I was providing the guy $3,000 at a time, many times a week, because the street medications were around $75 each pill.

But I was caught more times than I was successful. The UCLA doctor in charge of my case became frustrated with me and informed me that he would no longer assist me. I couldn't blame him—everyone was frightened of fentanyl in the tablets and me dying as a result of them. (When I arrived at the treatment center, I tested positive for fentanyl.)

This sickness... the dreadful thing. Addiction has damaged so much of my life that it's unfathomable. Relationships have been ruined as a result. It has wrecked my day-to-day existence. I have a friend who is poor and lives in a rent-controlled apartment. Never made it as an actress, has diabetes, is always concerned about money, and does not work. And I'd swap places with him in a heartbeat. In fact, I would give up all of my money, fame, and possessions to live in a rent-controlled apartment—I'd trade constantly worrying about money for not having this disease, this addiction.

And not only do I have the condition, but it is severe. In fact, I have it as terrible as it gets. It's always back-to-the-wall time. It'll kill me (I suppose something has to). When asked about his personal addiction, Robert Downey Jr. famously quipped, "It's like I have a gun in my mouth with my finger on the trigger, and I like the taste of the metal." I get it; I understand. Even on good days, when I'm sober and looking forward, it's always with me. There is still a weapon.

Fortunately, I believe there aren't enough opiates in the world to get me high. I have an extremely low bottom. Before I quit something, things have to get absolutely awful—big and horrific. I was virtually running the show Mr. Sunshine when I was doing it—writing it, acting in it. At home, I was taking notes for a writer on a script he had written. I had a bottle of vodka nearby. I made myself thirteen or fourteen drinks—but they were homemade, so triples. And I wasn't intoxicated after the fourteenth drink. So I stopped drinking.

I believe I'm now at the point with opiates where I'm in the same predicament. There simply aren't enough. In Switzerland, I took 1,800 mg of opiates per day and was not intoxicated. So, what shall I do? Call a drug dealer and demand all of the drugs? When I think of OxyContin, my imagination immediately jumps to having a colostomy bag for the rest of my life. That's something I couldn't manage. That's why I believe I'll be able to stay off opiates for the foreseeable future—they no longer work. And I could wake up after another operation, the fourteenth since the first, with an irreversible colostomy bag.

When I was taking fifty-five tablets a day, I would wake up and have to find those fifty-five pills. It was like doing a full-time job. Math was my entire life. I'll be there for three hours after I come home at eight o'clock. So I'm going to need four more. And then there's that dinner party. So I'll need seven.... And all for the sake of survival, of not becoming sick, of avoiding the unavoidable, which is the detox.

My mother and Keith Morrison were at the foot of my bed when we woke up one night after I had passed out and she had passed out. I wondered if I was in a Dateline episode. And if I am, why is my mother included?

My mother turned to face my girlfriend and said, "I think it's time for you to leave."

This literally saved my life.

My father has also saved my life several times.

I was glad for his being my father and doing the dad thing, but I also didn't want to be the source of the problem. They were simply going about their business; they had the number one hit TV show, and two of the key characters were set to marry. I couldn't just vanish. I simply wanted things to be alright. So I was transferred from Marina del Rey to Promises in Malibu and told that I would need more than twenty-eight days to recover—that I would need months.

A technician from Malibu drove me to the Friends set two weeks later. Jen Aniston remarked to me when I came, "I've been mad at you."

We hugged, and I went about my business. I married Monica and was transported back to the treatment center in a pickup truck led by a sober technician, at the peak of my highest point in Friends, the peak of my career, the famous moment on the classic show.
Let me tell you, not all the lights on Sunset that night were green.

I can't be effective in a relationship because I'm both trying to hold on and terrified of being abandoned. And that worry is unfounded, because in my fifty-three years and with all the lovely girlfriends I've had, I've only been abandoned once, many years ago. You'd think all the others I abandoned would outweigh this, but she was everything to me. But the wise man in me sees it clearly: she was just twenty-five and just trying to have fun; we dated for a few months, but I let all my barriers down. I resolved to be myself once and for all.

She then dumped me.

She had never made any promises to me. I was also drinking like a madman, which I don't blame her for.

I recently took a breath work class. You breathe in this extremely intense, very unpleasant way for half an hour. You cry, you see things, and you become high. It's the best type of free high for me. But Suboxone masks that sensation.... Half of the doctors I've spoken with believe I should be on Suboxone for at least a year, if not the rest of my life. Other doctors say I'm not officially sober as long as I'm on it. (It's very tough to get all the way off it anyway, which is odd considering it's a medicine designed to get you off other drugs. When I was hooked up to an IV of it recently, the dosage I was receiving was 0.5 lower than it should have been, and it made me nauseous and worried, so I had to increase it back up. When you stop taking it, you feel dreadful.)

When you take heroin, the substance hits your opiate receptors, and you get high, and then it fades and you're no longer hitting the opiate receptors, and you're sober for a time, and then maybe the next day you hit your opiate receptors again, and you get high, and so on. Suboxone, on the other hand, functions differently, attaching itself around the receptor and refusing to leave, essentially destroying your receptors 24/7.

I've seen God, of all places, in my kitchen, so I know there's something bigger than me. (For starters, I know I can't grow a plant.) I know it's an all-encompassing love and acceptance that says everything will be well. When you die, I'm sure something will happen. I'm sure you're on to something fantastic.

Alcoholics and addicts, like me, want to drink solely to feel better. That was certainly true for me: all I ever wanted was to feel better. I wasn't feeling well, so I had a couple of beers and felt better. However, as the sickness worsens, it takes more and more and more and more and more and more and more and more to feel better. If you pierce the sobriety membrane, alcoholism takes over and says, "Hey, remember me? It's good to see you again. Now, give me exactly what you gave me the last time, or I'll murder you or drive you insane." And then my mind's fixation sets in, and I can't stop thinking about feeling better, combined with a wanting phenomenon, and what you're left with is a bruise that starts out one way and never gets better. Nobody has a drinking issue, then stops, then drinks socially, and everything is OK. The sickness is just getting worse.

According to the Big Book, alcohol is devious, perplexing, and powerful... However, I would add that it is patient. When you raise your hand and say, "I'm having a problem," addiction responds, "Well, if you're going to be so stupid as to say something about it, I'll go away for a while..." I'll be in treatment for three months and say to myself, "Well, I'm going to use it when I get out of here, but I can wait nine more days." The sickness is simply tapping its fingers. It's often said in AA that when you're in a meeting, your sickness is outside doing one-armed push-ups, just waiting for you to leave.

I've come close to death countless times, and the lower you go on the scale (death is the lowest, FYI), the more people you can save. So, when my life is on fire, I have individuals I sponsor, people who call me to help them with their lives. From 2001 to 2003, I had two of the happiest years of my life—I was helping people, sober, and strong.

Addicts are not necessarily evil people. We're ordinary people trying to feel better, but we've got this condition. When I'm feeling down, I think to myself, "Give me something that will make me feel better." That's all there is to it. I would still like to drink and use drugs, but I don't because the repercussions would kill me.

I currently have numerous scars.

I fell into tears the first time I took my shirt off in my bathroom after returning from the hospital following my first operation. It really bothered me. I thought my life was coming to an end. After about a half-hour, I had the courage to phone my drug dealer, who proceeded to ask me what was wrong, as if he were a social worker or a priest, not a drug dealer.

I underwent my fourteenth operation three days ago—four years later. I cried once more. But I should get used to it since there will always be more surgeries—I will never be finished. I'll always have the bowels of a 90-year-old man. In fact, I've never gone through surgery without crying. Not even once.

But I've stopped calling the drug dealers.

My stomach is covered in scars, and all I have to do is look down to see that I've gone through a war, a self-inflicted war. Martin Sheen once turned to me at a Hollywood event—shirts were allowed, no, insisted on, thank God—and remarked, "Do you know what Saint Peter says to everyone who tries to get into heaven?" When I looked at him blankly, the former president added, "Peter says, 'Don't you have any scars?'" When most people would say triumphantly, 'Well, no, no, I don't,' Peter says, 'Why not? Was there nothing worthwhile to fight for?'"

I'd undergone a six-inch incision with metal staples in January 2022. This is the life of someone who has been given the big bad thing. And they won't let me smoke. It'll be a nice day if I don't smoke and nothing strange happens. When I don't smoke, I gain weight as well—in fact, I recently gained so much weight that I feared someone was following me when I glanced in the mirror.

You gain weight when you become sober. You gain weight after you stop smoking. Those are the guidelines.

I want to continue studying. I wish to continue teaching. Those are my lofty goals for myself, but in the meantime, I just want to laugh and have fun with my pals. I want to make love to a woman with whom I am deeply in love. I aspire to be a father and to make my mother and father proud.

I've accomplished a lot in my life, but there is still so much more to do, which excites me every day. I was a Canadian boy who had all of his dreams come true—but they were the wrong dreams. Instead of giving up, I adjusted and discovered new dreams.

I'm constantly finding them. They're right there in the Valley, on the edgings and flashes that reflect off the water when the sun hits... just so.

I see God when someone does something nice for someone else. But you can't give something away that you don't have. As a result, I strive to improve myself on a regular basis. When those times arrive and I'm needed, I've sorted out my issues and do what we're all here for: to serve others.

God and my therapist got together one day and decided to miraculously eliminate my desire to do drugs. A need that has plagued me since 1996.

My therapist's remarks touched home after having a colostomy bag for nine months. And when this man's comments hit home, the smart thing to do is to act quickly. What he said opened a tiny window, and I crawled through it. On the other hand, there was life without OxyContin.

I'd just had my fourteenth stomach surgery, to remove a hernia that had protruded through my abdominal wall. It had been excruciatingly painful, and I had been prescribed OxyContin. We addicts are not martyrs; if we are in severe agony, we are permitted to use pain medicine; however, this must be done with caution. This means that I never hold the bottle of pills, and the prescription is always administered by someone else, exactly as prescribed. It also meant I had a new scar on my stomach, a six-inch incision this time. Guys, are you serious? My colon burst, you opened me up to the extent that a bowling ball could fit inside, yet now I have the greatest scar?

My pain subsided immediately after the procedure, but something unexpected happened: I could feel my digestive tract locking up again. Anyone have PTSD? And when that happened, I went immediately to the emergency hospital, where I knew they'd either give me medication to help me pee or tell me I needed surgery right soon. And there was always the possibility that I may wake up with a colostomy bag if I had surgery. It had happened twice before, and it could happen again at any time.

And 7:00 a.m. the next day arrived way too quickly. My house was smoke-free, and I clutched to the vape for dear life. I remembered from past tries to quit that days three and four were the most difficult, but if I could make it to day seven, I'd be done.

It was every bit as bad as you might imagine. I essentially stayed in my room and vaped while waiting for the awful symptoms to pass. But I was courageous. This is something I could do.

I was 52 years old, and unless you're reading this for the first time, you already know that my intention was for the rest of my life to be both long and excellent. So I gave it a shot! I sat in my bed for nine days without smoking.

It was determined that dropping from sixty cigarettes per day to zero was too much for me to bear, and I would cut back on my smoking until a better strategy could be devised. I succeeded in reducing my weight from sixty to ten in the following days. Let's not forget: my life was on the line, and I needed that number to drop to zero as soon as possible. Any attempts to reduce the number to less than ten were futile.

Kerry's office was not what I expected from the world's most expensive hypnotist—it was cluttered with papers, photos, and anti nicotine signs. We sat down, and he began his "smoking is terrible " spiel—yeah, I know. Let's get down to business.

You're expected to keep smoking between meetings, which I appreciated, but to be gentle on my lungs and for Kerry's sake, I limited myself to ten cigarettes. (Anyone can smoke three packs a day, as I did, but you only need approximately ten cigarettes to acquire the nicotine your body wants. The other fifty are just habits.)

During the second session, Kerry used every fear tactic he could think of. I was foolish enough to believe that the next cigarette would not kill me. (No, I didn't.) I could have a cigarette right now, have a heart attack, and die if no one was nearby to call 911. My next cigarette could permanently damage my lungs, forcing me to spend the rest of my days carrying oxygen tanks and inhaling solely through my nose. (I thought to myself, "That's worse than a colostomy bag," but didn't say it aloud.) Would I rather smoke or breathe the next morning? (I already knew the answer.)

And then we arrived at our final meeting. This was it—I was going to stop smoking forever after this. I had told him that every time I tried to do this, I had failed miserably—it was more difficult to quit than narcotics. And, while quitting smoking, I did some really insane things (see under: head, wall). I'm frightened about withdrawal symptoms.

Sure, I smoked at least fifty times every day, but it was just a habit. I also observed that the wheezing had stopped. Kerry Gaynor had literally saved my life. I wasn't a smoker.

Another miracle had occurred. In fact, the miracles were flying around at breakneck speed—duck or you'll get hit by one. I don't want to do drugs and I don't smoke.

I had been smoke-free for fifteen days. I felt better, looked better, and needed less breaks during pickleball games. My eyes were full of life.

I practically started stalking Kerry Gaynor after that. I'd meet him whenever I could, buy a pack of smokes, enjoy one, and then wet the rest of the pack under the faucet. I never lied to Kerry—I always told him what was going on, and thankfully, he didn't kill the injured. I repeated all of the mantras and developed a strong phobia of smoking—a little fear with each inhale.

But I continued to smoke.

But I refused to give up—I couldn't. I deserve to smoke because my life has been so horrible. I deserve to smoke because I authored a script. These beliefs had to be instantly dismissed because they provided the addict hope.

I used to take 55 Vicodin every day and had quit, so I wasn't going to let this horrible, stinky, absolutely calming and delightful habit bring me down. Do I want to smoke or breathe? What a great thing we all take for granted: breathing.

Cigarettes had already made me really ill. They are also unhealthy. It may appear like I'm joking, but these are the things you must remember. I had to think about my comeback as an actor (I hadn't acted since my injury); I had a book to write and sell, and I couldn't do that with a cigarette in my hand. I couldn't just eat my way out of this either. "Stop drinking, using drugs, and smoking cigarettes!" Simply eat six chocolate cakes every night!" This was not the message I intended to send.

I needed to shatter a record: fifteen days. And with it, the soothing relief of not wanting to smoke. I've been there before, and I could do it again: a man's total reconstruction. I didn't know this man, but he seemed like a lovely guy who had finally quit beating the crap out of himself with a baseball bat.

I couldn't wait to find out who this dude was!

Chapter 11
Batman

I never believed I'd be fifty-two and single, not running around with very short, attractive kids repeating stupid sentences. I'd taught them all only to make my beautiful wife giggle.

For years, I felt inadequate, but that no longer holds true. I believe I am just the correct amount. However, every morning when I wake up, there are a few fleeting moments when I am blurry, lost to dreams and sleep, and don't know where I am, and I recall my stomach and the scar tissue that comes with it. (I finally have rock-hard abs, but they're not the result of sit-ups.) Then I swing my legs out of bed and tiptoe to the bathroom so I don't wake... Well, no one. Yes, sir, I am completely single. I examine myself in the bathroom mirror, hoping to find something that will explain everything. I try not to think about the amazing women I passed up because of a phobia that took me far too long to grasp. I try not to think about it too much because if you spend too much time gazing in the rearview mirror, you will crash your car. Still, I find myself yearning for a romantic companion. I'm not picky—five feet two, brunette, as sharp as a whip, humorous, and generally sane will suffice. She adores children. Hockey is tolerated. Willing to learn how to play pickleball.

I'm the newcomer this morning, like I am every morning out on the patio. I'm thrilled with, and inspired by, the "differences"—no alcohol, drugs, or smokes.... As I stand there, coffee in one hand and nothing in the other, watching the distant waves in the ocean, I realize I am experiencing my own wave within me.

Gratitude.

The wave of appreciation swelled as the light of day deepened and the water turned from silver to the palest aqua, till inside it I saw faces and events and little bits of flotsam that had been moments in my exciting life.

I was so fortunate to be alive, to have a loving family—this was not the least of my concerns, and probably the most important. I saw my mother's face in the water's thin spray and thought about her ineffable capacity to step up in a crisis, to take charge and make things better. (Keith Morrison once told me, "Throughout the four decades I've known your mother, her incredible attachment to you has been the center of her life." She is constantly thinking about you. When things become serious between us in 1980, she said something I'll never forget: "No man will ever come between Matthew and me—he'll always be the most important person in my life." That is something you will have to accept."' And it's true—there was never a time when I didn't feel loved. Even in our darkest hour. If something is seriously wrong, she is still my first point of contact.) I saw my father's extraordinarily attractive face as well, and it felt fitting that I saw him as both my father and the Old Spice sailor guy, though that last vision had long faded to a far point on the horizon. I think about how they were able to be in the same room with me when I was truly unwell, and what kind of love that betrays. They weren't meant to be together. That makes sense now. So I'd like to reclaim all the pennies I've put into wells, wishing they were all together. They both got lucky and married the individuals they were meant to marry.

My sisters' and brother's smiles echo my parents', each of them beaming at me not only at a hospital bedside, but also in Canada and Los Angeles as I tried to make them laugh with my patter. They never dropped the ball, and they never turned their backs on me. If you can, imagine such love.

It resulted in something significant for me. When I opened my eyes, I was surrounded by my Friends friends (without whom I would have starred in something called No Friends): Schwimmer, for making us stick together when he could have gone it alone and profited more than the rest, and deciding we should be a team and getting us a million dollars a week. No lady has ever made me laugh as hard as Lisa Kudrow. Courteney Cox, for convincing America that someone so attractive would marry someone like me. Jenny, thank you for allowing me to stare at that face for an extra two seconds every day. Matt LeBlanc, who transformed the show's only stock character into the funniest character. They were all still a phone call away. I was the one who sobbed the most during the reunion because I understood what I'd experienced, and the gratitude I felt then mirrors the gratitude I feel now. Beyond those ideals, there was the entire team, the producers, the writers, the performers, the audience members, so many happy smiles. Friends would have been a silent film without Marta Kauffman, David Crane, and Kevin Bright. ("Could this be more of a silent movie?") The fans, so many admirers who stuck with it and continue to watch—their faces stare back at me now, silent as God, as if I'm still on stage 24 in Burbank. Their laughter, which had given me purpose for so long, still resonates up these canyon walls, almost reaching me all these years later....

Erin is always present in the house when I need her. I don't tell her what I've been thinking about out there, but I see in her eyes that she might have an idea. She remains silent because that is what closest friends do. Erin, Erin, Erin, Erin... She saved my life in rehab when my insides exploded, and she continues to do so every day. Who knows what I'd do without her; I'm not going to find out. I can tell she's craving a cigarette, but she doesn't give in. Find a friend who will quit something with you—you'll be surprised at how much it improves your bond.

Life continues to go forward; each day is a new opportunity for amazement, hope, work, and forward motion. I'm curious if the A-list actress who has shown considerable interest in my new screenplay has yet to say yes....

I halt on the threshold as I walk inside. My life has been a series of portals between Canada and Los Angeles, Mom and Dad, L.A.X. 2194 and Friends, recovery and addiction, anguish and thankfulness, love and losing love. But I'm learning patience and getting a taste for reality. I return to the kitchen table and check my phone to see who has called. Not the A-lister, but there's still time.

This is how life is right now, and it's wonderful.

What kind of person am I going to be? Whoever it is, I will accept it as a man who has finally developed a taste for life. I battled that flavor like hell, man. But, in the end, admitting defeat won.

Addiction is far too powerful for anyone to overcome on their own. But we can beat it down one day at a time if we work together.

I got one thing right: I never gave up, never raised my hands and said, "That's enough, I can't take it anymore, you win." As a result, I now stand erect, ready for whatever comes next.

You, too, may be called upon to perform an important task someday, so be prepared.

And whatever happens, ask yourself, "What would Batman do?" then carry it out.

Printed in Great Britain
by Amazon

35934798R00066